Keto Bread

THE KETOGENIC COOKBOOK FOR YOUR LOW-CARB DIET WITH 100 RECIPES WHEAT AND GLUTEN-FREE RECIPES. (DELICIOUS MUFFINS, COOKIES, BUNS, ... BREAD LOAVES, PIZZA CRUSTS, & BREADSTICKS)

By
Susan Johnson

Contents

INTRODUCTION 1
KETO DIET 2
    THE PERCEPTION 2
    WHAT'S SO GREAT ABOUT KETOSIS ANYWAY? 4
    DOING IT RIGHT 6
    SUPPLEMENTATION 7
KETO BREAD RECIPE 9
    1. THE BEST KETO BREAD RECIPE 9
    2. EASY CLOUD BREAD (NO CREAM CHEESE, LACTOSE-FREE, LOW-CARB, KETO, PALEO) 12
    3. BUTTERY LOW CARB FLATBREAD 15
    4. CAULIFLOWER TORTILLAS 17
    5. 15-MINUTE GLUTEN FREE, LOW CARB & KETO TORTILLAS 19
    6. CAULIFLOWER BREAD RECIPE WITH GARLIC & HERBS - LOW CARB GARLIC BREAD 22
    7. GARLIC & HERB FOCACCIA {GRAIN FREE & LOW CARB} 25
    8. ROSEMARY AND GARLIC COCONUT FLOUR BREAD 28
    9. KETO MACADAMIA BREAD 30
    10. LOW CARB PALEO ALMOND FLOUR BISCUITS RECIPE (GLUTEN-FREE) - 4 INGREDIENTS 32
    11. KETO BAGEL RECIPE 34
    12. KETO CRANBERRY ORANGE BREAD 36
    13. (15 MINUTE!) GLUTEN FREE & KETO PIZZA CRUST 39
    14. HEALTHY 3 INGREDIENT MINI PALEO PIZZA BASES CRUSTS 42
    15. KETO ZUCCHINI BREAD WITH WALNUTS 45
    16. CHEESY SKILLET BREAD 47
    17. 3 INGREDIENT PALEO NAAN (INDIAN BREAD) 50
    18. THE BEST KETO DINNER ROLLS 52
    19. NUT-FREE KETO BUNS 55
    20. CHEESY KETO GARLIC BREAD - USING MOZZARELLA DOUGH 58
    21. COCONUT FLOUR PSYLLIUM HUSK BREAD - PALEO 60
    22. GLUTEN FREE, PALEO & KETO BREAD 62
    23. 90 SECOND MICROWAVE BREAD 2.7 NET CARBS 66

24.	Rosemary and Garlic Coconut Flour Bread	68
25.	Cranberry Feta Dough Balls	70
26.	Jalapeno Low Carb Bagel	72
27.	Keto Cheddar Bay Biscuits - Red Lobster biscuits copycat recipe	74
28.	Keto Fathead Bagels	76
29.	Keto Blueberry Lemon Bread	78
30.	Keto Banana Bread	81
31.	Ultimate Dairy-Free Keto Bread	84
32.	Cheesy Garlic Bread Muffins	86
33.	Keto Low Carb Buns with Psyllium Husk	88
34.	Coconut Flour Mini Cheese Loaves	91
35.	Low Carb Keto Garlic Breadsticks	93
36.	Keto Zucchini Bread	96
37.	Keto Fiber Bread Rolls Recipe	98
38.	Almond Flour Bread	100
39.	Rosemary Olive Bread	102
40.	Keto Cream Cheese Bread	104
41.	Cheddar Garlic Fathead Rolls	107
42.	Coconut Flour Pizza Crust	109
43.	Low Carb Blueberry English Muffin Bread Loaf	111
44.	Keto Pumpkin Bread	113
45.	Cranberry Jalapeño "Cornbread" Muffins	116
46.	3 Minute Low Carb Biscuits	118
47.	Coconut flour flatbread	119
48.	Easy Paleo Keto Bread Recipe - 5 Ingredients	122
49.	Coconut Bread	125
50.	Collagen Keto Bread	126
51.	Keto Breakfast Pizza	128
52.	Paleo Chocolate Zucchini Bread	129
53.	Low-Carb Focaccia Bread with Thyme and Onion	132
54.	Cheesy Skillet Bread	133
55.	Keto Flax Seed Bread	135
56.	Keto Mini Bread Loaves	136

57.	Low Carb Asparagus Egg Bites	138
58.	Cheesy Low Carb Biscuits	140
59.	Grain Free Irish Soda Bread (Low Carb and Sugar-Free)	142
60.	Low Carb Carrot Cake Muffins	143
61.	Sweet Keto Challah Bread Recipe	145
62.	Low Carb Focaccia Bread	147
63.	Soul Bread Sesame Rolls	149
64.	Keto Pull Apart Clover Rolls	151
65.	Low Carb Bagels-Gluten Free Onion Sesame	153
66.	Keto + Low Carb Cornbread Muffins	155
67.	Easy Low Carb Cheese Bombs	157
68.	Sunflower Pumpkin Seed Psyllium Bread	158
69.	1-2-3 Bread (Dairy-Free)	160
70.	Simple and Fluffy Gluten-Free Low-Carb Bread	161
71.	Keto Paleo Low-Carb Stuffing	162
72.	Low Carb Paleo Tortillas Recipe - 3 Ingredient Coconut Flour Wraps	164
73.	Paleo Gluten-Free Low Carb English Muffin Recipe in a Minute	166
74.	Low Carb Chelsea Buns	168
75.	Cinnamon Raisin Swirl Bread	170
76.	Keto Cheddar Bay Biscuits	173
77.	Parmesan & Tomato Keto Bread Buns	175
78.	Keto Croissants	177
79.	Cinnamon Almond Flour Bread {Paleo}	179
80.	Low Carb Gluten Free Cranberry Bread	181
81.	Rosemary Keto Bagels	183
82.	Homemade Nut and Seed Paleo Bread	184
83.	Keto Low Carb Mug Bread	186
84.	Garlic, Dill & Cheddar Keto Bread	187
85.	Low Carb Pumpkin Bread	190
86.	Buttery Low Carb Flatbread	192
87.	Peanut Butter Berry Breakfast Loaf (Low Carb, Gluten Free)	193
88.	Hot Ham and Cheese Roll-Ups with Dijon Butter Glaze	195
89.	Low Carb Hot Cross Buns	197

90.	Monkey Bread	199
91.	Low Sugar Gluten Free Pumpkin Bread	201
92.	Lemon Poppy Seed Loaf Cake	202
93.	Broccoli & Cheddar Keto Bread Recipe	204
94.	Turmeric Cauliflower Buns	206
95.	Low Carb Keto Banana Walnut Bread	208
96.	3-Ingredient Grain-Free Bagels	210
97.	Nearly No Carb Keto Bread	211
98.	Keto Walnut Bread	213
99.	Gluten Free, Paleo & Keto Drop Biscuits	214
100.	Turmeric Cauliflower Buns	217

CONCLUSION **219**

INTRODUCTION

Simply, our body, organs, muscles, and brain can use either glucose or ketones for fuel. It is the function of the liver and pancreas (primarily) to regulate that fuel supply and they show a strong bias toward sticking with glucose. Glucose is the 'preferred' fuel because it is derived in abundance from the diet and readily available readily from liver and muscle stores. Ketones have to be deliberately synthesized by the liver, but the liver can easily synthesize glucose (a process known as 'gluconeogenesis' that uses amino acids (protein) or other metabolic intermediaries) too.

Following a low carb diet doesn't have to mean lettuce-wrapped sandwiches for life! With this quick bread recipe, you can have French toast or grilled cheese sandwiches without sacrificing your carb count.

The secret to creating a light and airy keto bread that can hold up to the toaster is using plenty of eggs and healthy fat. Ghee is a butterfat that is cooked longer to filter out the milk solids, which makes it much easier on the digestive system for people with lactose sensitivities.

I discovered that picking the right keto bread for your needs really depends on what you're craving at the moment. A quick-and-simple bread isn't going to have the crumb or structure of a more labor-intensive one. Some recipes are great for grilled cheese but would fall apart if subjected to the juicy heft of a burger.

Keto Diet

A keto diet is defined as eating in a way for your body to produce ketones. Ketones are produced by the liver from fat and that process is triggered by eating very little carbohydrates and a decent amount of protein. The ketones are used by the body for energy. Thus, a keto diet essentially burns fat as the body's source of fuel. The fat is burned nonstop by your body. When your body produces ketones, it moves into a state of ketosis. The ketosis will burn fat without even worrying about fasting. That is, as long as you keep eating a ketogenic diet.

Ketogenic Diets (more specifically Cyclic Ketogenic Diets) are the most effective diets for achieving rapid, ultra low bodyfat levels with maximum muscle retention! Now, as with all such general statements there are circumstantial exceptions. But done right - which they rarely are - the fat loss achievable on a ketogenic diet is nothing short of staggering! And, despite what people might tell you, you will also enjoy incredible high energy and overall sense of well being.

The Perception

Despite these promises, more bodybuilders/shapers have had negative experiences than have seen positive results. The main criticisms are:
- Chronic lethargy
- Unbearable hunger
- Massive decrease in gym performance
- Severe muscle loss

All of these criticisms result from a failure to heed the caveat above: Ketogenic Diets must be done right! It must be realized that they are an entirely unique metabolic modality that adheres to none of the previously accepted 'rules' of dieting. And there is no going half-way; 50 grams of carbs per day plus high protein intake is NOT ketogenic!

So how are ketogenic diets 'done right'? Lets quickly look at how they work.

We don't get beta-hydroxybutyrate, acetone, or acetoacetate (ketones) from the diet. The liver synthesizes them only under duress; as a last measure in conditions of severe glucose deprivation like starvation. For the liver to be convinced that ketones are the order of the day, several conditions must be met:

- Blood glucose must fall below 50mg/dl
- Low blood glucose must result in low Insulin and elevated Glucagon
- Liver glycogen must be low or 'empty'
- A plentiful supply of gluconeogenic substrates must NOT be available

At this point it is important to mention that it is not actually a question of being 'in' or 'out' of ketosis; we don't either totally run on ketones, or not. It is a gradual and careful transition so that the brain is constantly and evenly fuelled... ideally. Ketones SHOULD be produced in small amounts from blood glucose levels of about 60mg/dl. We consider ourselves in ketosis when there are greater concentrations of ketones than glucose in the blood.

The reality is that most people - especially weight trainers - have had a regular intake of glucose for a good couple of decades, at least. The liver is perfectly capable of producing ketones but the highly efficient gluconeogenic pathways are able to maintain low-normal blood glucose above the ketogenic threshold.

Couple this with the fact that many people are at least partially insulin resistant and have elevated fasting insulin (upper end of the normal range, anyway). The small amount of blood glucose from gluconeogenesis induces sufficient insulin release to blunt glucagon output and the production of ketones.

Sudden glucose deprivation will have the consequence, initially, of lethargy, hunger, weakness, etc in most people - until ketosis is achieved. And Ketosis will not be reached until the liver is forced to quit with gluconeogenesis and start producing ketones. As long as dietary protein is sufficient then the liver will continue to produce glucose and not ketones. That's why no carb, high protein diets are NOT ketogenic.

What's So Great About Ketosis Anyway?

When the body switches over to running primarily on ketones a number of very cool things happen:

- Lipolysis (bodyfat breakdown) is substantially increased
- Muscle catabolism (muscle loss) is substantially reduced
- Energy levels are maintained in a high and stable state
- Subcutaneous fluid (aka 'water retention') is eliminated

Basically, when we are in ketosis our body is using fat (ketones) to fuel everything. As such, we aren't breaking down muscle to provide glucose. That is, muscle is being spared because it has nothing to offer; fat is all the body needs (well, to a large extent). For the dieter, this means substantially less muscle loss than what is achievable on any other diet. Make sense?

As a bonus, ketones Serving only 7 calories per gram. This is higher than the equal mass of glucose but substantially less (22%, in fact) than the 9 calorie gram of fat from whence it came. We like metabolic inefficiencies like this. They mean we can eat more but the body doesn't get the calories.

Even cooler is that ketones cannot be turned back into fatty acids; the body excretes any excess in the urine! Speaking of which, there will be quite a bit of urine; the drop in muscle glycogen, low Insulin, and low aldosterone all equate to massive excretion of intra and extracellular fluid. For us that means hard, defined muscularity and quick, visible results.

Regarding energy, our brain actually REALLY likes ketones so we tend to feel fantastic in ketosis - clear-headed, alert and positive. And because there is never a shortage of fat to supply ketones, energy is high all the time. Usually, you even sleep less and wake feeling more refreshed when in ketosis.

Doing it Right

From whats said above you will realize that to get into ketosis:

- Carbohydrate intake should be nil; Zero!
- Protein intake should be low - 25% of calories at a maximum
- Fat must account for 75%+ of calories

With low insulin (due to zero carbs) and calories at, or below maintenance, the dietary fat cannot be deposited in adipose tissues. The low-ish protein means that gluconeogenesis will quickly prove inadequate to maintain blood glucose and, whether the body likes it or not, there is still all the damned fat to burn.

And burn it does. The high dietary fat is oxidized for cellular energy in the normal fashion but winds up generating quantities of Acetyl-CoA that exceed the capacity of the TCA cycle. The significant result is ketogenesis - synthesis of ketones from the excess Acetyl-CoA. In more lay terms: the high fat intake "forces" ketosis upon the body. This is how it's done right'.

Now you just have to throw out what you thought was true about fats. Firstly, fat does not "make you fat". Most of the information about the evils of saturated fats, in particular, is so disproportionate or plain wrong anyway; on a ketogenic diet, it is doubly inapplicable. Saturated fats make ketosis fly. And don't worry; your heart will be better than fine and your insulin sensitivity will NOT be reduced (there is no insulin around in the first place)!

Once in ketosis, it is not necessary, technically speaking, to maintain absolute zero carbs or low protein. But it is still better if you want to reap the greatest rewards. Besides, assuming you are training hard, you will still want to follow a cyclic ketogenic diet where you get to eat all your carbs, fruit and whatever else, every 1-2 weeks.

Don't be mistaken; 'done right' does not make ketogenic dieting easy or fun for the culinary acrobats among you. They are probably the most restrictive diets you can use and not an option if you don't love animal products. Get out your Nutrition Infoal almanac and work out an 20:0:80 protein:carb: fat diet. Yeah, it's boring. As an example, your writers daily ketogenic diet is 3100 Calories at 25:0.5:74.5 from only:

- 10 XXL Whole Eggs
- 160ml Pure Cream (40% fat)
- 400g Mince (15% fat)
- 60ml Flaxseed Oil
- 30g Whey Protein Isolate

Supplementation

There are a number of supplements that assist in making Ketogenic diets more effective. However, many popular supplements would be wasted. Here is an overview of the main ones:

- Chromium and ALA, while not insulin 'mimickers' as many claims, increase insulin sensitivity resulting in lower insulin levels, higher glucagon, and a faster descent into deeper ketosis

- creatine is a bit of a waste - at most, 30% can be taken up by the muscles that, without glycogen, cannot be meaningfully 'volumized'.
- HMB (if it works) would/should be an excellent supplement for minimizing the catabolic period before ketosis is achieved
- Tribulus is excellent and comes highly recommended as it magnifies the increased testosterone output of a ketogenic diet
- Carnitine in L or Acetyl-L form is an almost essential supplement for Ketogenic Diets. L-Carnitine is necessary for the formation of Ketones in the liver.
- Glutamine, free-form essential and branched-chain aminos are worthwhile for pre and post training. Just don't overdo the glutamine as it supports gluconeogenesis
- ECA stack fat burners are very useful and important though don't worry about the inclusion of HCA
- Flaxseed oil is great but does not think that you need 50% of your calories from essential fatty acids. 1-10% of calories is more than sufficient.
- Whey Protein is optional - you don't want too much protein remember
- A soluble fiber supplement that is non-carbohydrate based is good. But walnuts are easier.

Keto Bread Recipe

1. The Best Keto Bread Recipe

Prep Time 10 mins
Cook Time 1 hr 5 mins
Total Time 1 hr 15 min
Servings: 10

Ingredients

- 1 1/4 cups (5oz/143g) almond flour
- 5 tablespoons psyllium husk*powder
- 2 teaspoons baking powder
- 1 teaspoon salt
- 2 teaspoons apple cider vinegar
- 1 cup (8floz/225ml) boiling water
- 3 egg whites
- 2 tablespoons sesame seeds, optional

Instructions

- Pre-heat your oven to 350°F (180°C) then butter and line a 9x5 inch loaf tin with parchment paper. Set aside.

- In a large bowl combine the almond flour, psyllium husk*, baking powder and salt.

- Add the egg whites and apple cider vinegar to the dry ingredients with an electric mixer on medium speed until a paste-like dough is formed.

- While mixing on low speed, stream in the boiling water. Turn the speed up to high and mix for about 30 seconds, or until the dough forms and elastic play-dough like mixture. Be careful not to over-mix!

- Transfer the dough to the prepared baking tin and smooth the top. Lastly, sprinkle over the sesame seeds.

- Bake the bread for 55-65 minutes or until the top has risen and puffed up like a traditional sandwich loaf.

- Remove the bread from the oven and allow to cool slightly before transferring to a cooling rack.

- Once cooled slice and enjoy! Store the bread covered at room temperature for 2 days. After 2 days I suggest storing it in the fridge for no longer than another 2 days.

Recipe Notes

If for some reason you can't find psyllium husk, you can substitute ground flax or flax meal.

Nutrition Info

Calories 53 Calories from Fat 27
Total Fat 3g 5%
Sodium 55mg 2%
Potassium 37mg 1%
Total Carbohydrates 4g 1%
Dietary Fiber 6g 24%
Protein 2g 4%

2. Easy Cloud Bread (NO Cream cheese, lactose-free, low-carb, Keto, Paleo)

This oopsie bread is perfect for dairy-free peeps! No cream cheese at all, instead I'm using coconut cream for the same fluffy turnout. These are perfect to make a low carb sandwich, mini pizza, or burger bun!

Prep Time 15 mins
Cook Time 20 mins
Total Time 35 mins
Servings: 10 pieces
Calories: 36 kcal

Ingredients

- 3 eggs
- 3 tbsp coconut cream spoon from refrigerated can of full-fat coconut milk
- 1/2 tsp baking powder
- optional toppings: sea salt black pepper and rosemary or whatever seasonings you like!

Instructions

- Firstly, prep everything. Once you start going, you'll need to move quickly so have everything handy. Pre-heat the oven to 325f degrees and arrange a rack in the middle. Line a baking sheet with parchment paper and set aside. Grab your tools: hand mixer (you can use a stand mixer, but I find it to be better for whipping egg whites so I can stay in control), all ingredients, any additional seasonings, two mixing bowls (the larger one should be used for egg whites), a large spoon to scoop and drop the bread with.

- Using a full-fat can of coconut milk that has been refrigerated overnight or several hours, spoon out the top coconut cream and add to the smaller bowl.

- Separate eggs into the two bowls, adding the yolk to the bowl with the cream and be careful to not let the yolk get into the whites in the larger bowl.

- Using a hand mixer, beat the yolk and cream together first until nice and creamy, make sure there are no clumps of coconut left.

- Wash your whisks well and dry them.

- Add the baking powder into the whites and start beating on medium with the hand mixer for a few minutes, moving around and you'll see it get firmer. Keep going for a few minutes, you want to get it as thick as you can with stiff peaks. The thicker the better. Just don't over-do it. Once you can stop and dip the whisks in leaving peaks behind, you're ready.

- Quickly and carefully add the yolk-coconut mixture into the whites, folding with a spatula, careful not to deflate too much. Keep going until everything is well combined but still fluffy.

- Now you can grab your spoon and start dropping your batter down on the baking sheet. Keep going as quickly and carefully as you can, or it will start to melt. They should look pillow-y.

- Steadily add your baking sheet to the middle rack in the oven and bake for approx. 20-25 minutes. You should be able to scoop them up with your spatula and see a fluffy top and a flat bottom. Store in the fridge for about a week or freeze.

3. Buttery Low Carb Flatbread

The best thing since sliced bread. Mostly because it's gluten-free, fried, and slathered in butter.

Prep time 5 mins
Cook time 2 mins
Total time 7 mins
Serves: 4

Ingredients

- 1 cup Almond Flour
- 2 tbsp Coconut Flour
- 2 tsp Xanthan Gum
- ½ tsp Baking Powder
- ½ tsp Falk Salt + more to garnish
- 1 Whole Egg + 1 Egg White
- 1 tbsp Water
- 1 tbsp Oil for frying
- 1 tbsp melted Butter-for slathering

Instructions

- Whisk together the dry ingredients (flours, xanthan gum, baking powder, salt) until well combined.
- Add the egg and egg white and beat gently into the flour to incorporate. The dough will begin to form.
- Add the tablespoon of water and begin to work the dough to allow the flour and xanthan gum to absorb the moisture.
- Cut the dough in 4 equal parts and press each section out with cling wrap. Watch the video for instructions!
- Heat a large skillet over medium heat and add oil.
- Fry each flatbread for about 1 min on each side.
- Brush with butter (while hot) and garnish with salt and chopped parsley.

Nutrition Info

Serving size: 1 flatbread; Calories: 232; Fat: 19; Carbohydrates: 9; Fiber: 5; Protein: 9

4. Cauliflower Tortillas

Great low carb alternative to traditional corn or flour tortillas.
Prep Time 30 minutes
Cook Time 20 minutes
Total Time 50 minutes
Servings 6 tortillas
Calories 37

Ingredients

- 3/4 large head cauliflower (or two cups riced)
- 2 large eggs (Vegans, sub flax eggs)
- 1/4 cup chopped fresh cilantro

- 1/2 medium lime, juiced and zested
- salt & pepper, to taste

Instructions

- Preheat the oven to 375 degrees F., and line a baking sheet with parchment paper.
- Trim the cauliflower, cut it into small, uniform pieces, and pulse in a food processor in batches until you get a couscous-like consistency. The finely riced cauliflower should make about 2 cups packed.
- Place the cauliflower in a microwave-safe bowl and microwave for 2 minutes, then stir and microwave again for another 2 minutes. If you don't use a microwave, a steamer works just as well. Place the cauliflower in a fine cheesecloth or thin dishtowel and squeeze out as much liquid as possible, being careful not to burn yourself. Dishwashing gloves are suggested as it is very hot.
- In a medium bowl, whisk the eggs. Add in cauliflower, cilantro, lime, salt and pepper. Mix until well combined. Use your hands to shape 6 small "tortillas" on the parchment paper.
- Bake for 10 minutes, carefully flip each tortilla, and return to the oven for an additional 5 to 7 minutes, or until completely set. Place tortillas on a wire rack to cool slightly.
- Heat a medium-sized skillet on medium. Place a baked tortilla in the pan, pressing down slightly, and brown for 1 to 2 minutes on each side. Repeat with remaining tortillas.

5. 15-Minute Gluten Free, Low Carb & Keto Tortillas

These 15-minute gluten free and keto tortillas are super pliable, easy and make the best low carb Mexican tacos!

Prep Time: 10 minutes
Cook Time: 5 minutes
Total Time: 15 minutes
Servings: 4

Ingredients

- 96 g almond flour
- 24 g coconut flour
- 2 teaspoons xanthan gum

- 1 teaspoon baking powder
- 1/8-1/4 teaspoon kosher salt depending on whether sweet or savory
- 2 teaspoons apple cider vinegar
- 1 egg lightly beaten
- 3 teaspoons water

Instructions

- Add almond flour, coconut flour, xanthan gum, baking powder and salt to food processor. Pulse until thoroughly combined.

- Pour in apple cider vinegar with the food processor running. Once it has distributed evenly, pour in the egg. Followed by the water. Stop the food processor once the dough forms into a ball. The dough will be sticky to touch.

- Wrap dough in cling film and knead it through the plastic for a minute or two. Think of it a bit like a stress ball. Allow dough to rest for 10 minutes (and up to two days in the fridge).

- Heat up a skillet (preferably) or pan over medium heat. You can test the heat by sprinkling a few water droplets, if the drops evaporate immediately your pan is too hot. The droplets should 'run' through the skillet.

- Break the dough into eight 1" balls (26g each). Roll out between two sheets of parchment or waxed paper with a rolling pin or using a tortilla press (easier!) until each round is 5-inches in diameter.

- Transfer to skillet and cook over medium heat for just 3-6 seconds (very important). Flip it over immediately (using a thin spatula or knife), and continue to cook until just lightly golden on each side (though with the traditional charred marks), 30 to 40 seconds. The key is not to overcook them, as they will no longer be pliable or puff up.

- Keep them warm wrapped in kitchen cloth until serving. To rewarm, heat briefly on both sides, until just warm (less than a minute).

- These tortillas are best eaten straight away. But feel free to keep some dough handy in your fridge for up to three days.

Nutrition Info

Calories 89 Calories from Fat 54
Total Fat 6g 9%
Saturated Fat 1g 5%
Cholesterol 20mg 7%
Sodium 51mg 2%
Potassium 58mg 2%
Total Carbohydrates 4g 1%
Dietary Fiber 2g 8%
Protein 3g 6%

6. Cauliflower Bread Recipe with Garlic & Herbs - Low Carb Garlic Bread

This cauliflower bread loaf with garlic & herbs makes a keto, paleo, low carb garlic bread that's healthy & delicious! Great for low carb sandwiches, too.

Prep Time 15 minutes
Cook Time 45 minutes
Total Time 1 hour

Ingredients

- 3 cup Cauliflower ("riced" using food processor*)
- 10 large Egg (separated)
- 1/4 tsp Cream of tartar (optional)
- 1 1/4 cup Coconut flour
- 1 1/2 tbsp Gluten-free baking powder
- 1 tsp Sea salt
- 6 tbsp Butter (unsalted, measured solid, then melted; can use ghee for dairy-free)
- 6 cloves Garlic (minced)
- 1 tbsp Fresh rosemary (chopped)
- 1 tbsp Fresh parsley (chopped)

Instructions

- Preheat the oven to 350 degrees F (177 degrees C). Line a 9x5 in (23x13 cm) loaf pan with parchment paper.

- Steam the riced cauliflower. You can do this in the microwave (cooked for 3-4 minutes, covered in plastic) OR in a steamer basket over water on the stove (line with cheesecloth if the holes in the steamer basket are too big, and steam for a few minutes). Both ways, steam until the cauliflower is soft and tender. Allow the cauliflower to cool enough to handle.

- Meanwhile, use a hand mixer to beat the egg whites and cream of tartar until stiff peaks form.

- Place the coconut flour, baking powder, sea salt, egg yolks, melted butter, garlic, and 1/4 of the whipped egg whites in a food processor.

- When the cauliflower has cooled enough to handle, wrap it in kitchen towel and squeeze several times to release as much moisture as possible. (This is important - the end result should be very dry and clump together.) Add the cauliflower to the food processor. Process until well combined. (Mixture will be dense and a little crumbly.)

- Add the remaining egg whites to the food processor. Fold in just a little, to make it easier to process. Pulse a few times until just incorporated. (Mixture will be fluffy.) Fold in the chopped parsley and rosemary. (Don't overmix to avoid breaking down the egg whites too much.)

- Transfer the batter into the lined baking pan. Smooth the top and round slightly. If desired, you can press more herbs into the top (optional).

- Bake for about 45-50 minutes, until the top is golden. Cool completely before removing and slicing.

- How To Make Buttered Low Carb Garlic Bread (optional): Top slices generously with butter, minced garlic, fresh parsley, and a little sea salt. Bake in a preheated oven at 450 degrees F (233 degrees C) for about 10 minutes. If you want it more browned, place under the broiler for a couple of minutes.

Nutrition Info

Calories 108; Fat 8g; Protein 6g; Total Carbs 8g; Net Carbs 3g; Fiber 5g; Sugar 3g

7. Garlic & Herb Focaccia {Grain Free & Low Carb}

Quit bread for good and get this grain free focaccia on your plate.

Prep time 10 mins
Cook time 20 mins
Total time 30 mins
Serves: 8 slices

Ingredients

Dry Ingredients
- 1 cup Almond Flour
- ¼ cup Coconut Flour
- ½ tsp Xanthan Gum
- 1 tsp Garlic Powder
- 1 tsp Flaky Salt

- ½ tsp Baking Soda
- ½ tsp Baking Powder

Wet Ingredients

- 2 eggs
- 1 tbsp Lemon Juice
- 2 tsp Olive oil + 2 tbsp Olive Oil to drizzle

Top with Italian Seasoning and TONS of flaky salt!

Instructions

- Heat oven to 350 and line a baking tray or 8-inch round pan with parchment.
- Whisk together the dry ingredients making sure there are no lumps.
- Beat the egg, lemon juice, and oil until combined.
- Mix the wet and the dry together, working quickly, and scoop the dough into your pan.
- ***Make sure not to mix the wet and dry until you are ready to put the bread in the oven because the leavening reaction begins once it is mixed!!!
- Smooth the top and edges with a spatula dipped in water (or your hands) then use your finger to dimple the dough. Don't be afraid to go deep on the dimples! Again, a little water keeps it from sticking.
- Bake covered for about 10 minutes. Drizzle with Olive Oil bake for an additional 10-15 minutes uncovering to brown gently.

- Top with more flaky salt, olive oil (optional), a dash of Italian seasoning and fresh basil. Let cool completely before slicing for optimal texture!!

Notes

3g Net Carbs per big long slice.

You can also cut it into squares and you'd just want to adjust how many servings you get vs the macros1

Nutrition Info
- Serving size: 1
- Calories: 166
- Fat: 13
- Carbohydrates: 7
- Fiber: 4
- Protein: 7

8. Rosemary and Garlic Coconut Flour Bread

Prep Time: 10 minutes
Cook Time: 45 minutes
Total Time: 55 minutes
Servings: 10 Slices

Ingredients

- 1/2 cup Coconut flour
- 1 stick butter (8 tbsp)
- 6 large eggs
- 1 tsp Baking powder
- 2 tsp Dried Rosemary

- 1/2-1 tsp garlic powder
- 1/2 tsp Onion powder
- 1/4 tsp Pink Himalayan Salt

Instructions

- Combine dry ingredients (coconut flour, baking powder, onion, garlic, rosemary and salt) in a bowl and set aside.
- Add 6 eggs to a separate bowl and beat with a hand mixer until you get see bubbles at the top.
- Melt the stick of butter in the microwave and slowly add it to the eggs as you beat with the hand mixer.
- Once wet and dry ingredients are fully combined in separate bowls, slowly add the dry ingredients to the wet ingredients as you mix with the hand mixture.
- Grease an 8x4 loaf pan and pour the mixture into it evenly.
- Bake at 350 for 40-50 minutes (time will vary depending on your oven).
- Let it rest for 10 minutes before removing from the pan. Slice up and enjoy with butter or toasted!

Nutrition Info

- Calories: 147kcal
- Carbohydrates: 3.5g
- Protein: 4.6g
- Fat: 12.5g
- Fiber: 2g

9. Keto Macadamia Bread

Prep Time: 15 minutes
Cook Time: 45 minutes
Serving: 8

Ingredients

- 1 cup macadamia nuts
- 1/4 cup almond flour
- 2 scoops grass-fed whey protein powder
- 2 tbsp ground flax seeds
- 1 tsp baking soda
- 3/4 tsp himalayan salt
- 4 eggs
- 2 egg whites
- 1/4 cup grass-fed ghee, melted
- 1 tbsp apple cider vinegar

Instructions

- Preheat the oven to 350 F. Rub the bottom of your loaf pan with ghee or extra virgin olive oil to prevent sticking.
- In a food processor, pulse the macadamia nuts for about 30-45 seconds or until it creates a flour consistency.
- Add the almond flour, whey protein, flax seeds, baking soda, and himalayan salt to the food processor. Continue to pulse until ingredients are mixed well.
- In a medium size bowl beat eggs, egg whites, melted ghee and apple cider vinegar with a whisk.
- Fold in dry ingredients.
- Pour into a greased loaf pan and bake for approximately 45 minutes.

Nutrition Info

- Calories per serving: 262
- Fat per serving: 23g
- Carbs per serving: 4g
- Protein per serving: 12g
- Fiber per serving: 2g
- Sugar per serving: 1g (added sugar: 0g)
- Sodium per serving: 417mg

10. Low Carb Paleo Almond Flour Biscuits Recipe (Gluten-free) - 4 Ingredients

This paleo almond flour biscuits recipe needs just 4 common ingredients & 10 minutes prep. These buttery delicious low carb biscuits will become your favorite!

Prep Time 10 minutes
Cook Time 15 minutes
Total Time 25 minutes

Ingredients

- 2 cup Blanched almond flour
- 2 tsp Gluten-free baking powder
- 1/2 tsp Sea salt
- 2 large Egg (beaten)
- 1/3 cup Butter (measured solid, then melted; can use ghee or coconut oil for dairy-free)

Instructions

- Preheat the oven to 350 degrees F (177 degrees C). Line a baking sheet with parchment paper.
- Mix dry ingredients together in a large bowl. Stir in wet ingredients.
- Scoop tablespoonfuls of the dough onto the lined baking sheet (a cookie scoop is the fastest way). Form into rounded biscuit shapes (flatten slightly with your fingers).
- Bake for about 15 minutes, until firm and golden. Cool on the baking sheet.

Nutrition Info

- Calories 164
- Fat 15g
- Protein 5g
- Total Carbs 4g
- Net Carbs 2g
- Fiber 2g
- Sugar 1g

11. Keto Bagel Recipe

Missing a good bagel in your Keto lifestyle? Now you don't have to!

Prep Time: 5 minutes
Cook Time: 25 minutes
Serving: 2

Ingredients

- 1 cup (120 g) of almond flour
- 1/4 cup (28 g) of coconut flour
- 1 Tablespoon (7 g) of psyllium husk powder

- 1 teaspoon (2 g) of baking powder
- 1 teaspoon (3 g) of garlic powder
- pinch salt
- 2 medium eggs (88 g)
- 2 teaspoons (10 ml) of white wine vinegar
- 2 1/2 Tablespoons (38 ml) of ghee, melted
- 1 Tablespoon (15 ml) of olive oil
- 1 teaspoon (5 g) of sesame seeds

Instructions

- Preheat the oven to 320°F (160°C).
- Combine the almond flour, coconut flour, psyllium husk powder, baking powder, garlic powder and salt in a bowl.
- In a separate bowl, whisk the eggs and vinegar together. Slowly drizzle in the melted ghee (which should not be piping hot) and whisk in well.
- Add the wet mixture to the dry mixture and use a wooden spoon to combine well. Leave to sit for 2-3 minutes.
- Divide the mixture into 4 equal-sized portions. Using your hands, shape the mixture into a round shape and place onto a tray lined with parchment paper. Use a small spoon or apple corer to make the center hole.
- Brush the tops with olive oil and scatter over the sesame seeds. Bake in the oven for 20-25 minutes until cooked through. Allow to cool slightly before enjoying!

Nutrition Info

Calories: 629; Sugar: 4 g; Fat: 56 g; Carbohydrates: 19 g; Fiber: 12 g; Protein: 19 g

12. Keto Cranberry Orange Bread

This recipe makes a keto cranberry orange bread. It's a low carb quick bread that features the flavors of fresh cranberries and orange zest and extract.

Prep Time: 10 minutes
Cook Time: 1 hour
Additional Time: 10 minutes
Total Time: 1 hour 20 minutes
Serving: 12

Ingredients

Keto Cranberry Orange Bread Batter
- 2 1/2 cups of finely milled almond flour
- 1 cup of sugar substitute

- 2 teaspoons of baking powder
- 1/2 teaspoon of sea salt
- 8 whole eggs
- 8 ounces of room temperature full-fat cream cheese
- 2 teaspoons of orange extract
- 1/2 cup of room temperature unsalted butter
- 2 cups of fresh or frozen whole cranberries
- 1 tablespoon of orange zest

Keto Orange Glaze

- 3/4 cup of confectioners sugar substitute
- 3 tablespoons of freshly squeezed lemon juice
- 2 tablespoons of heavy whipping cream
- 1 teaspoon of orange extract
- 2 teaspoons of orange zest

Instructions

Keto Cranberry Orange Bread

- Preheat oven to 350 degrees.
- Grease and line with parchment paper a 10 inch loaf pan or two 6 inch loaf pans. (note if using two smaller pans check for doneness at 35 minute mark)
- In a medium-sized bowl measure then sift the almond flour. To the sifted flour add the baking powder, sea salt and stir. Set this aside.
- In a large bowl using an electric hand-held mixer or stand-up mixer blend the butter, cream cheese, and sugar-substitute until mixture is light fluffy.

- Next add the eggs one at a time, making sure to scrape the bowl several times.
- To the wet batter add the dry ingredients and combine until well-incorporated.
- Fold in the cranberries in the bread batter.
- Spread the batter into the greased loaf pan.
- Bake for 60-70 minutes or until an inserted toothpick comes out clean.
- Allow the loaf to cool in the pan for about 30 minutes before taking it out of the pan. Then let the pan cool on a baking rack for another 30 minutes before adding the icing or freezing.

Keto Orange Icing

- In a small mixing bowl whisk the confectioners sugar substitute, lemon juice, orange zest, orange extract and heavy cream. Stir until fully combined.
- Spread/drizzle the icing over the cooled keto cranberry bread.
-

Nutrition Info

- Calories: 337
- Total Fat: 30.6g
- Saturated Fat: 11.4g
- Cholesterol: 154mg
- Sodium: 157mg
- Carbohydrates: 6.9g
- Fiber: 3.2g
- Sugar: 1.9g
- Protein: 10.3g

13. (15 Minute!) Gluten Free & Keto Pizza Crust

Looking for a quick and easy keto pizza? This (15-minute!!) gluten free, dairy free and keto stove top pizza crust is most definitely for you!

Prep Time: 10 minutes
Cook Time: 5 minutes
Total Time: 15 minutes
Servings: slices
Calories: 118 kcal

Ingredients

For the keto pizza dough:
- 96 g almond flour

- 24 g coconut flour
- 2 teaspoons xanthan gum
- 2 teaspoons baking powder
- 1/4 teaspoon kosher salt depending on whether sweet or savory
- 2 teaspoons apple cider vinegar
- 1 egg lightly beaten
- 5 teaspoons water as needed

Topping suggestions:

- our keto marinara sauce
- mozzarella cheese
- pepperoni or salami
- fresh basil
-

Instructions

For the keto dough:

- Add almond flour, coconut flour, xanthan gum, baking powder and salt to food processor. Pulse until thoroughly combined.
- Pour in apple cider vinegar with the food processor running. Once it has distributed evenly, pour in the egg. Followed by the water, adding just enough for it to come together into a ball. The dough will be sticky to touch from the xanthan gum, but still sturdy.
- Wrap dough in plastic wrap and knead it through the plastic for a minute or two. Think of it a bit like a stress ball. The dough should be smooth and not significantly cracked (a couple here and there are fine). In which case get it back to the food processor and add in more water 1 teaspoon at a time. Allow

dough to rest for 10 minutes at room temperature (and up to 5 days in the fridge).
- If cooking on the stove top: heat up a skillet or pan over medium/high heat while your dough rests (you want the pan to be very hot!). If using the oven: heat up a pizza stone, skillet or baking tray in the oven at 350°F/180°C. The premise is that you need to blind cook/bake the crust first on both sides without toppings on a very hot surface.
- Roll out dough between two sheets of parchment paper with a rolling pin. You can play with thickness here, but we like to roll it out nice and thin (roughly 12 inches in diameter) and fold over the edges (pressing down with wet fingertips).
- Cook the pizza crust in your pre-heated skillet or pan, top-side down first, until blistered (about 2 minutes, depending on your skillet and heat). Lower heat to medium/low, flip over your pizza crust, add toppings of choice and cover with a lid. Alternatively you can always transfer it to your oven on grill to finish off the pizza.
- Serve right away. Alternatively, note that the dough can be kept in the fridge for about 5 days. So you can make individual mini pizzettes throughout the week.

Nutrition Info

Calories 118 Calories from Fat 81; Total Fat 9g 14%
Saturated Fat 1.3g 7%; Cholesterol 27mg 9%
Sodium 116mg 5%; Potassium 10mg 0%
Total Carbohydrates 5.5g 2%; Dietary Fiber 3g 12%
Sugars 0.8g; Protein 5g 10%

14. Healthy 3 Ingredient Mini Paleo Pizza Bases Crusts

These 3 Ingredient mini paleo pizza crusts or bases are an easy, delicious and low carb alternative to traditional pizzas! Made with just three ingredients and on the stovetop, these 3 Ingredient Pizza bases are naturally gluten free, grain free, high protein, low calorie and have a nut free option!

Servings: 4
Calories: 125kcal

Ingredients

For the coconut flour option

- 8 large egg whites for thicker bases, use 5 whole eggs and 3 egg whites
- 1/4 cup coconut flour sifted
- 1/2 tsp baking powder
- Spices of choice salt, pepper, Italian spices
- Extra coconut flour to dust very lightly

For the almond flour option

- 8 large egg whites
- 1/2 cup almond flour
- 1/2 tsp baking powder
- Spices of choice salt, pepper, Italian spices

For the pizza sauce

- 1/2 cup Mutti tomato sauce
- 2 cloves garlic crushed
- 1/4 tsp sea salt
- 1 tsp dried basil

Instructions

To make the pizza bases/crusts

- In a large mixing bowl, whisk the eggs/egg whites until opaque. Sift in the coconut flour or almond flour and whisk very well until clumps are removed. Add the baking powder, mixed spices and continue to whisk until completely combined.
- On low heat, heat up a small pan and grease lightly.

- Once frying pan is hot, pour the batter in the pan and ensure it is fully coated. Cover the pan with a lid/tray for 3-4 minutes or until bubbles start to appear on top. Flip, cook for an extra 2 minutes and remove from pan- Keep an eye on this, as it can burn out pretty quickly.
- Continue until all the batter is used up.
- Allow pizza bases to cool. Once cool, use a skewer and poke holes roughly over the top, for even cooking. Dust very lightly with a dash of coconut flour.

To make the sauce

- Combine all the ingredients together and let sit at room temperature for at least 30 minutes- This thickens up.

Notes

For a crispy pizza base, bake in the oven for 3-4 minutes prior to adding your toppings.If you want to freeze them, allow pizza bases to cool completely before topping with a dash of coconut flour and a thin layer of pizza sauce. Ensure each pizza base is divided with parchment paper before placing in the freezer.

Nutrition Info

Calories: 125kcal; Carbohydrates: 6g; Protein: 8g; Fat: 1g; Fiber: 3g; Vitamin A: 1%; Vitamin C: 2%; Calcium: 1%; Iron: 2%

15. Keto Zucchini Bread with Walnuts

Servings: 4

Ingredients

- 3 large eggs
- ½ cup olive oil
- 1 teaspoon vanilla extract
- 2 ½ cups almond flour
- 1 ½ cups erythritol
- ½ teaspoon salt
- 1 ½ teaspoons baking powder
- ½ teaspoon nutmeg
- 1 teaspoon ground cinnamon
- ¼ teaspoon ground ginger
- 1 cup grated zucchini
- ½ cup chopped walnuts

Instructions

- Preheat oven to 350°F. Whisk together the eggs, oil, and vanilla extract. Set to the side.
- In another bowl, mix together the almond flour, erythritol, salt, baking powder, nutmeg, cinnamon, and ginger. Set to the side.
- Using a cheesecloth or paper towel, take the zucchini and squeeze out the excess water.
- Then, whisk the zucchini into the bowl with the eggs.
- Slowly add the dry ingredients into the egg mixture using a hand mixer until fully blended.
- Lightly spray a 9×5 loaf pan, and spoon in the zucchini bread mixture.
- Then, spoon in the chopped walnuts on top of the zucchini bread. Press walnuts into the batter using a spatula.
- Bake for 60-70 minutes at 350°F or until the walnuts on top look browned.

Nutrition Info

- 200.13 Calories
- 18.83g Fats
- 2.6g Net Carbs
- 5.59g Protein.

16. Cheesy Skillet Bread

Easy low carb skillet bread with a wonderful crust of cheddar cheese. This keto bread recipe is perfect with soups and stews, and makes the BEST low carb Thanksgiving stuffing!

Prep Time 10 mins
Cook Time 16 mins
Total Time 26 mins
Servings: 10

Ingredients

- 1 tbsp butter for the skillet
- 2 cups almond flour
- 1/2 cup flax seed meal
- 2 tsp baking powder
- 1/2 tsp salt
- 1 & 1/2 cups shredded Cheddar cheese divided
- 3 large eggs lightly beaen
- 1/2 cup butter melted
- 3/4 cup almond milk

Instructions

- Preheat oven to 425F. Add 1 tbsp butter to a 10-inch oven-proof skillet and place in oven.
- In a large bowl, whisk together almond flour, flax seed meal, baking powder, salt and 1 cup of the shredded cheddar cheese.
- Stir in the eggs, melted butter and almond milk until thoroughly combined.
- Remove hot skillet from oven (remember to put on your oven mitts), and swirl butter to coat sides.
- Pour batter into pan and smooth the top. Sprinkle with remaining 1/2 cup cheddar.
- Bake 16 to 20 minutes, or until browned around the edges and set through the middle. Cheese on top should be nicely browned.
- Remove and let cool 15 minutes.

Recipe Notes

Serves 10. Each serving has 7.2 g of carbs and 4 g of fiber. Total NET CARBS = 3.2 g.

Nutrition Info

Calories 357 Calories from Fat 276
Total Fat 30.63g 47%
Total Carbohydrates 7.9g 3%
Dietary Fiber 4.77g 19%
Protein 12.48g 25%

17.3 Ingredient Paleo Naan (Indian bread)

Prep Time: 5 minutes Serving: 6 small naans Method: Stovetop Cuisine: Indian

Ingredients

- ½ cup almond flour
- ½ cup tapioca flour or arrowroot flour
- 1 cup coconut milk, canned and full fat
- Salt, adjust to taste, optional
- Ghee (slather that bread!), optional

Instructions

- Preheat a crepe pan OR nonstick pan over medium heat.
- Mix all the ingredients together in a bowl, and pour ¼ cup of the batter onto the pan.
- After the batter fluffs up and looks firm/mostly cooked, flip it over to cook the other side (be patient, this takes a little time!).
- Serve immediately or cool on a wire rack.

Notes

Options for Size:

- If your naan is a bit sticky in the middle, you can put it on a baking sheet and bake for 5 minutes at 350F or for 10-15 minutes at 400F for a crispier flatbread.
- If you want to make a dessert crepe, pour the batter and spread it out as thin as you can.
- If you are not using a non-stick pan, you will need to use some sort of oil/ghee/fat to keep the batter from sticking. I have and love this carbon steel crepe pan.
- If the cream has solidified in your canned coconut milk, then mix well before using.

Nutrition Info

Calories Per Serving: 129
15% Total Fat 9.6g
0% Cholesterol 0mg
0% Sodium 6mg
4% Total Carbohydrate 11g
Sugars 1.4g
2% Protein 1g

18. The Best Keto Dinner Rolls

These are the best keto dinner rolls to help replace bread in your low carb lifestyle. This recipe is easy, filling, and delicious!

Prep Time: 5 minutes
Cook Time: 10 minutes
Total Time: 15 minutes
Serving: 6 rolls

Ingredients

- 1 Cup Mozzarella, shredded
- 1 oz Cream Cheese
- 1 Cup Almond Flour
- 1/4 Cup Ground Flax Seed
- 1 egg
- 1/2 Tsp Baking Soda

Instructions

- Preheat oven to 400
- Line baking sheet with parchment, set aside
- In a medium bowl, melt cream cheese and mozzarella together (microwave ~1 min)
- Stir cheeses together until smooth, add egg and stir until combined
- In separate bowl combine almond flour, ground flax seed and baking soda
- Mix cheese and egg mixture into dry ingredients and stir until dough forms soft ball (it will be sticky)
- Using wet hands, gently roll dough into 6 balls

- Roll tops in sesame seeds if desired and place onto lined baking sheet
- Bake for 10-12 minutes until golden brown
- Let cool for 15 minutes

Notes

- Coconut flour is NOT a direct substitute for almond flour, you must adjust the amount

- Dough will be sticky but should be able to form balls. Use wet hands to roll balls. If absolutely too wet to mold then add an additional tbsp of almond flour until pliable

- 4 large rolls work great for sandwiches and burgers, 6 smaller is good for dinner rolls

Nutrition Info

- Serving Size: 1 roll
- Calories: 219
- Fat: 18g
- Carbohydrates: 5.6g total (2.3g NET)
- Fiber: 3.3g
- Protein: 10.7g

19. Nut-Free Keto Buns

Hands-on 10-15 minutes
Overall 1 hour 15 minutes
Serving: 10 buns

Ingredients

Dry ingredients

- 1 1/4 cup fine defatted sesame seed flour (100 g / 3.5 oz)
- 2/3 cup flaxmeal (100 g / 3.5 oz)
- 2/3 cup coconut flour (80 g / 2.8 oz)
- 1/3 packed cup psyllium husk powder (40 g / 1.4 oz)
- 2 tsp garlic powder
- 2 tsp onion powder
- 2 tsp cream of tartar or apple cider vinegar
- 1 tsp baking soda

- 1 tsp salt (pink Himalayan or sea salt)
- 5 tbsp sesame seeds (or sunflower, flax, poppy seeds) or 1-2 tbsp caraway seeds for topping

Wet ingredients

- 6 large egg whites
- 2 large eggs
- 2 1/4 - 2 1/2 cups water depending on the consistency, boiling or lukewarm depending on the method - see intro (540 ml / 18 fl oz) - Use only 2 cups if using ground sesame seeds / sesame seed meal instead of defatted sesame seed flour.

Instructions

- Preheat the oven to 175 °C/ 350 °F. Use a kitchen scale to measure all the ingredients carefully. I used defatted sesame seed flour but you can try sesame seed meal instead and use less water. To make sesame seed meal, I just blend the seeds until powdered (just like I do with flax seeds to make flax meal).
- I used Sukrin sesame flour (UK) but you can use this brand too (US) - both should be defatted. Nut-Free Keto Buns
- Mix all the dry ingredients apart from the seeds for the topping in a bowl: sesame flour, coconut flour, flaxmeal, psyllium powder, ...
- Do not use whole psyllium husks - if you cannot find psyllium husk powder, use a blender or coffee grinder and process until fine. If you get already prepared psyllium husk powder, remember to weigh it before adding to the recipe. I used whole psyllium husks which I grinded myself. Do not use just measure cups - different products have different weights per cup! Nut-Free
- ..., baking soda, cream of tartar, garlic powder, ...

- Cream of tartar and baking soda act as leavening agents. This is how it works: To get 2 teaspoons of gluten-free baking powder, you need 1/2 a teaspoon of baking soda and 1 teaspoon of cream of tartar (double in this recipe of 10 buns). If you don't have cream of tartar, instead you can use apple cider vinegar and add it to the wet ingredients. Nut-Free Keto Buns
- ... onion powder and salt
- Add the egg whites and eggs and process well using a mixer until the dough is thick.
- Nut-Free Keto Buns The reason you shouldn't use only whole eggs is that the buns wouldn't rise with so many egg yolks in. Don't waste them - use them for making Home-made Mayo, Easy Hollandaise Sauce or Lemon Curd.
- Add boiling water and mix until well combined. Nut-Free Keto Buns
- Using a spoon or hands, form the buns and place them on a non-stick baking tray or a parchment paper. They will grow in size as they bake, so make sure to leave some space between them. Top each of the buns with sesame seeds (or any other seeds) and press them into the dough, so they don't fall out.
- Place in the oven and cook for 55-60 minutes. Remove from the oven, let the tray cool down and place the buns on a rack to cool down to room temperature. Store them at room temperature if you plan to use them in the next couple of days or in the freezer for future use.
- Top with butter or cream cheese, burger meat and meat-free toppings. Enjoy!

Nutrition Info

Net carbs3.5 grams; Protein12.3 grams; Fat10.6 grams; Calories180 kcal

20. Cheesy Keto Garlic Bread - using mozzarella dough

The BEST recipe for cheesy keto garlic bread - using mozzarella dough. At only 1.5g net carbs per slice, this is an absolute keeper for your low-carb recipe folder.

Prep Time 10 mins
Cook Time 15 mins
Total Time 25 mins
Servings: 10

Ingredients

- 170 g pre shredded/grated cheese mozzarella
- 85 g almond meal/flour
- 2 tbsp cream cheese full fat
- 1 tbsp garlic crushed
- 1 tbsp parsley fresh or dried

- 1 tsp baking powder
- pinch salt to taste
- 1 egg medium

Instructions

- Place all the ingredients apart from the egg, in a microwaveable bowl. Stir gently to mix together. Microwave on HIGH for 1 minute.
- Stir then microwave on HIGH for a further 30 seconds.
- Add the egg then mix gently to make a cheesy dough.
- Place on a baking tray and form into a garlic bread shape. Cut slices into the low-carb garlic bread.
- Optional: Mix 2 tbsp melted butter, 1 tsp parsley and 1 tsp garlic. Brush over the top of the low-carb garlic bread, sprinkle with more cheese.
- Bake at 220C/425F for 15 minutes, or until golden brown.

Nutrition Info

Calories 117.4 Calories from Fat 88
Total Fat 9.8g 15%
Total Carbohydrates 2.4g 1%
Dietary Fiber 0.9g 4%
Sugars 0.6g
Protein 6.2g 12%

21. Coconut Flour Psyllium Husk Bread - Paleo

Want an easy low carb keto Paleo bread? Try this gluten free coconut flour psyllium bread recipe. It's a tasty bread to serve with breakfast or dinner.

Prep Time 5 minutes
Cook Time 55 minutes
Total Time 1 hour
Servings 15 slices
Calories 127kcal

Ingredients

- 6 tablespoons whole psyllium husks 27g, may want to finely grind
- 3/4 cup warm water
- 1 cup coconut flour 125g
- 1 1/2 teaspoons baking soda
- 3/4 teaspoon sea salt

- 1 pint egg whites 2 cups (or use 8 whole eggs)
- 2 large eggs see note
- 1/2 cup olive oil
- 1/4 cup coconut oil melted

Instructions

- Preheat oven to 350°F.
- If not using silicone pan, grease or line pan with parchment paper. I used an 8x4-in pan.
- Dump all ingredients into a food processor and pulse until well combined. If you don't have a food processor, you can use a mixing bowl with electric mixer.
- Spread batter into 8x4 loaf pan. Smooth top.
- Bake for 45-55 minutes or until edges are brown and toothpick inserted comes out clean.
- Let bread sit in pan for 15 minutes. Remove bread from pan and allow to cool completely on rack.

Nutrition Info

Calories 127 Calories from Fat 120
Total Fat 13.3g 20%
Sodium 243mg 10%
Total Carbohydrates 6g 2%
Dietary Fiber 4.1g 16%
Protein 3g 6%

22. Gluten Free, Paleo & Keto Bread

Count on this paleo and keto bread to be soft, fluffy, absolutely delicious and with a killer crumb. Plus, with less than half the amount of eggs as your usual low carb bread recipe, this non-eggy sandwich bread will surely become a staple!

Prep Time: 15 minutes
Cook Time: 30 minutes
Resting Time: 40 minutes
Total Time: 45 minutes
Servings: 1
Calories: 174 kcal

Ingredients

For the paleo & keto bread

- 2 teaspoons active dry yeast
- 2 teaspoons maple syrup or honey, to feed the yeast (NO SUGAR WILL BE REMAIN POST BAKE)
- 120 ml water lukewarm between 105-110°F
- 168 g almond flour
- 83 g golden flaxseed meal finely ground
- 15 g whey protein isolate
- 18 g psyllium husk finely ground
- 2 teaspoons xanthan gum or 4 teaspoons ground flaxseed meal
- 2 teaspoons baking powder
- 1 teaspoon kosher salt
- 1/4 teaspoon cream of tartar

- 1/4 teaspoon ground ginger
- 1 egg at room temperature
- 110 g egg whites about 3, at room temperature
- 56 g grass-fed butter or ghee, melted and cooled
- 1 tablespoon apple cider vinegar
- 58 g sour cream or coconut cream + 2 tsp apple cider vinegar

Instructions

For the paleo & keto bread

- Line a 8.5 x 4.5 inch loaf pan with parchment paper (an absolute must!). Set aside.
- Add yeast and maple syrup (to feed the yeast, see notes) to a large bowl. Heat up water to 105-110°F, and if you don't have a thermometer it should only feel lightly warm to touch. Pour water over yeast mixture, cover bowl with a kitchen towel and allow to rest for 7 minutes. The mixture should be bubbly, if it isn't start again (too cold water won't activate the yeast and too hot will kill it).
- Mix your flours while the yeast is proofing. Add almond flour, flaxseed meal, whey protein powder, psyllium husk, xanthan gum, baking powder, salt, cream of tartar and ginger to a medium bowl and whisk until thoroughly mixed. Set aside.
- Once your yeast is proofed, add in the egg, egg whites, lightly cooled melted butter (you don't want to scramble the eggs or kill the yeast!) and vinegar. Mix with an electric mixer for a couple minutes until light and frothy. Add the flour mixture in two batches, alternating with the sour cream, and mixing until thoroughly incorporated. You want to mix thoroughly and quickly to activate the xanthan gum, though the dough will become thick as the flours absorb the moisture.

- Transfer bread dough to prepared loaf pan, using a wet spatula to even out the top. Cover with a kitchen towel and place in a warm draft-free space for 50-60 minutes until the dough has risen just past the top of the loaf pan. How long it takes depends on your altitude, temperature and humidity- so keep an eye out for it every 15 minutes or so. And keep in mind that if you use a larger loaf pan it won't rise past the top.
- Preheat oven to 350°F/180°C while the dough is proofing. And if you're baking at high altitude, you'll want to bake it at 375°F/190°C.
- Place the loaf pan over a baking tray and transfer gently into the oven. Bake for 45-55 minutes until deep golden, covering with a lose foil dome at minute 10-15 (just as it begins to brown). Just be sure that the foil isn't resting directly on the bread.
- Allow the bread to rest in the loaf pan for 5 minutes and transfer it to a cooling rack. Allow to cool completely for best texture- this is an absolute must, as your keto loaf will continue to cook while cooling! Also keep in mind that some slight deflating is normal, don't sweat it!
- Keep stored in an airtight container (or tightly wrapped in cling film) at room temperature for 4-5 days, giving it a light toast before serving. Though you'll find that this keto bread is surprisingly good even without toasting!

Recipe Notes

- Before you scream sugar (got 5 emails about it right after posting!!) remember that the yeast will feed on such sugar to emit carbon dioxide, so it doesn't affect the carb count at all. And yes, this is a scientific fact.

- If paleo (or in keto maintenance), feel free to sub 1/4 to 1/2 cup of almond flour with arrowroot flour for a lighter crumb.

Nutrition Info

- Calories 174 Calories from Fat 126
- Total Fat 14g 22%
- Saturated Fat 3g 15%
- Cholesterol 26mg 9%
- Sodium 254mg 11%
- Potassium 83mg 2%
- Total Carbohydrates 6g 2%
- Dietary Fiber 4g 16%
- Protein 5g 10%

23. 90 Second Microwave Bread 2.7 net carbs

This 90 second bread is made in the microwave and you can use almond flour or coconut flour.

Prep Time: 3 minutes
Cook Time: 2 minutes
Total Time: 5 minutes
Servings: 1

Ingredients

- 3 tbsp almond flour or 1 1/3 tbsp coconut flour
- 1 tbsp oil (melted butter, melted coconut oil, avocado oil)
- 1/2 tsp baking powder
- 1 large egg
- tiny pinch of salt

Instructions

- Add all ingredients to a 4x4 microwave safe bowl, tap on the counter a few times to remove air bubbles, and microwave for 90 seconds. You can also bake in a oven safe container for 10 minutes at 375F
- Tap the container on the counter a few times to remove any air bubbles before you cook it
- You could really use any nut flour that you want if you are allergic to almonds or coconut. For alternative nut flours like pecan four, you would use 3 tbsp. You use half the amount for coconut flour because it's not really a nut and it is very absorbent!

- I found that a 4x4 microwave safe container made the perfect size piece of low carb bread that could be cut in half and stuffed with all the things
- You could also use a round container that is 4 inches in diameter for a keto mug bread
- If you would rather bake this in the oven, you can use an oven safe container and bake at 375 for 10 minutes
- Toasting this low carb bread makes it have a much better texture. you could also use a skillet to toast it in some butter. Yum!

Nutrition Info

Calories: 315kcal

24. Rosemary and Garlic Coconut Flour Bread

Prep Time: 10 minutes
Cook Time: 45 minutes
Total Time: 55 minutes
Servings: 10 Slices

Ingredients

- 1/2 cup Coconut flour
- 1 stick butter (8 tbsp)
- 6 large eggs
- 1 tsp Baking powder
- 2 tsp Dried Rosemary
- 1/2-1 tsp garlic powder
- 1/2 tsp Onion powder
- 1/4 tsp Pink Himalayan Salt

Instructions

- Combine dry ingredients (coconut flour, baking powder, onion, garlic, rosemary and salt) in a bowl and set aside.
- Add 6 eggs to a separate bowl and beat with a hand mixer until you get see bubbles at the top.
- Melt the stick of butter in the microwave and slowly add it to the eggs as you beat with the hand mixer.
- Once wet and dry ingredients are fully combined in separate bowls, slowly add the dry ingredients to the wet ingredients as you mix with the hand mixture.
- Grease an 8x4 loaf pan and pour the mixture into it evenly.

- Bake at 350 for 40-50 minutes (time will vary depending on your oven).
- Let it rest for 10 minutes before removing from the pan. Slice up and enjoy with butter or toasted!

Nutrition Info

- Calories: 147kcal
- Carbohydrates: 3.5g
- Protein: 4.6g
- Fat: 12.5g
- Fiber: 2g

25. Cranberry Feta Dough Balls

Festive low carb dough balls with cranberry & feta

Prep Time: 15 minutes
Cook Time: 35 minutes
Total Time: 50 minutes
Servings: 4 People

Ingredients

- 1 cup mozzarella cheese grated
- 1/2 cup parmesan cheese grated
- 1/2 cup coconut flour
- 2 eggs beaten
- 1 cup Feta cheese crumbled
- 3 tablespoons cranberry chia jam
- 1/4 cup butter, melted unsalted
- 1/2 teaspoon baking powder
- 2 tablespoons chives, chopped optional garnish

Instructions

- Preheat the oven to 200C/400 degrees.
- In a bowl, mix the Mozzarella and Parmesan cheese together.
- Add the eggs and butter and mix thoroughly.
- Add the coconut flour and baking powder and mix until you almost have a dough like texture.
- Add the Feta cheese and cranberry chia jam, gently mixing this throughout the dough.

- Using your hands (clean!) make 15 even shaped balls for the tree shape. Anything left over can be used as the trunk if need be.
- Place the balls on a parchment covered baking tin in the shape of a Christmas Tree. You could try a festive wreath too!
- Bake for 30-35 until firm and golden.

Nutrition Info

- Calories: 121kcal
- Carbohydrates: 3.7g
- Protein: 6g
- Fat: 9g
- Fiber: 1.9g

26. Jalapeno Low Carb Bagel

Prep Time: 10 minutes
Cook Time: 30 minutes
Total Time: 40 minutes
Servings: 6 Bagels
Calories: 273kcal

Ingredients

- 2 cups Mozzarella cheese grated
- 2 oz Cream cheese
- 1 cup Almond flour
- 1 teaspoon baking powder
- 3 Jalapeno peppers
- 2 Eggs
- 1 oz Cheddar cheese grated

Instructions

- Preheat the oven to 200C/400F
- Chop and deseed the jalapeno peppers. Slice a few thin circles and set them aside for the decoration.
- In a bowl, mix the almond flour and baking powder.
- Add the chopped jalapeno peppers and eggs. Mix well.
- In another bowl add the mozzarella and cream cheese.
- Cook in the microwave for 2 minutes, stopping after 1 minute to give it a gentle stir (you'll end up with crispy bits around the bowl otherwise).
- Remove and stir, then add in the almond flour mixture.
- Stir well and combine until you have a blended dough.

- Break the dough up into 6 pieces and roll out the pieces to make into a bagel shape OR use a donut tray to place the dough in. (I find this easier to keep them neater).
- Decorate the bagels with sliced jalapenos and sprinkle with some grated Cheddar cheese.
- Bake for 20-30 minutes, keeping an eye on them that they bake until golden.
- Eat and enjoy!

Nutrition Info

- 273 Calories
- 22g Fat
- 16g Protein
- 6g Total Carb
- 2g Fibre
- 4g Net Carbs

27. Keto Cheddar Bay Biscuits - Red Lobster biscuits copycat recipe

These keto cheddar bay biscuits taste so much like Red Lobster biscuits! Try this copycat recipe for savory, cheesy, and EASY keto dinner rolls.

Prep time: 5 mins
Cook time: 25 mins
Total time: 30 mins

Ingredients:

- 2 cups almond flour (what we used)
- 2 teaspoons baking powder
- 1/2 teaspoon Himalayan salt
- 1/2 teaspoon garlic powder
- 1/4 teaspoon ground black pepper
- 4 tablespoons grass-fed unsalted butter, chilled and cut into small pieces
- 4 tablespoons heavy whipping cream
- 2 large eggs, beaten
- 4 ounces white cheddar cheese, shredded
- 2 ounces sharp yellow cheddar cheese, shredded
- 1 tablespoon dried parsley

Instructions

- Preheat oven to 350 degrees. Line a baking sheet with parchment or a silicone baking liner.
- In a large mixing bowl, blend all dry ingredients. Add butter and crumble with a fork (or your hands, if they're cold) until incorporated well into the dry mix.
- Add heavy cream in small amounts, mixing well between each addition. Stir eggs into the mixture. Mix white cheddar into the batter until it forms a doughy consistency, then gently add in yellow cheddar.
- Scoop 8 even portions of dough onto your prepared baking sheet. (You can also roll into balls instead if you want rounder biscuits.)
- Bake for 20 minutes, or until browned on the bottom.
- Serve warm, or cool completely and store in a covered container. Reheat gently in a toaster oven when ready to serve again.

Nutrition Info

- Calories 350
- Fat (grams) 32
- Sat. Fat (grams) 12
- Carbs (grams) 6.2
- Net carbs 3.1
- Protein (grams) 13
- Sugar (grams) 1.4
- Fiber (in grams) 3.1

28. Keto Fathead Bagels

Truly chewy keto bagels - you want them and I've got them! These bagels are low carb, nut-free, and take only 5 ingredients to make. Easy and delicious, they will take your healthy breakfast to a whole new level.

Prep Time 20 mins
Cook Time 20 mins
Total Time 40 mins
Servings: 8 servings

Ingredients

- 1/2 cup coconut flour (56g)
- 2 tsp baking powder
- 3/4 tsp xanthan gum
- 12 oz pre-shredded part skim mozzarella
- 2 large eggs

Optional Topping for Everything Bagels

- 1 tsp sesame seeds
- 1 tsp poppyseed
- 1 tsp dried minced onion
- 1/2 tsp coarse salt
- 1 tbsp butter melted

Instructions

- Preheat the oven to 350F and line a large baking sheet with a silicone liner. In a medium bowl, whisk together the coconut flour, baking powder, and xanthan gum. Set aside.
- In a large microwave safe bowl, melt the cheese on high in 30 second increments until well melted and almost liquid. Stir in the flour mixture and the eggs and knead in the bowl using a rubber spatula.
- Turn out onto the prepared baking sheet and continue to knead together until cohesive. Cut the dough in half and cut each half into 4 equal portions so that you have 8 equal pieces of dough.
- Roll each portion out into a log about 8 inches long. Pinch the ends of the log together.
- In a shallow dish, stir together the sesame seeds, poppyseed, dried onion, and salt. Brush the top of each bagel with melted butter and dip firmly into the everything seasoning. Set back on the silicone mat.
- Bake 15 to 20 minutes, until the bagels have risen and are golden brown.

Nutrition Info

- Calories 190 Calories from Fat 111
- Total Fat 12.3g 19%
- Total Carbohydrates 5.5g 2%
- Dietary Fiber 2.6g 10%
- Protein 12.1g 24%

29. Keto Blueberry Lemon Bread

This recipe for keto blueberry bread is grain-free, gluten-free, sugar-free, low carb and it's diabetic and keto-friendly. If that's not enough it also happens to be easy to make.

Prep Time: 10 minutes
Cook Time: 1 hour
Additional Time: 15 minutes
Total Time: 1 hour 25 minutes
Serving: 12

Ingredients

Keto Blueberry Lemon Bread Batter

- 2 1/2 cups of finely milled almond flour
- 1 cup of sugar substitute
- 2 teaspoons of baking powder
- 1/2 teaspoon of sea salt
- 8 whole eggs
- 8 ounces of room temperature full-fat cream cheese
- 2 teaspoons of lemon extract
- 1/2 cup of room temperature unsalted butter
- 2 cups of fresh or frozen whole blueberries
- 1 tablespoon of lemon zest

Keto Lemon Glaze

- 3/4 cup of confectioners sugar substitute
- 3 tablespoons of freshly squeezed lemon juice

- 2 tablespoons of heavy whipping cream
- 1 teaspoon of lemon extract
- 2 teaspoons of lemon zest

Instructions

Keto Blueberry Lemon Bread

- Preheat oven to 350 degrees.
- Grease and line with parchment paper a 10X5 inch loaf pan or two 6 inch loaf pans. (note if using two smaller pans check for doneness at 35 minute mark)
- In a medium-sized bowl measure then sift the almond flour. To the sifted flour add the baking powder, sea salt and stir. Set this aside.
- In a large bowl using an electric hand-held mixer or stand-up mixer blend the butter, cream cheese, and sugar-substitute until mixture is light fluffy.
- Next add the 8 eggs one at a time, making sure to scrape the bowl several times.
- To the wet batter add the dry ingredients and combine until well-incorporated.
- Fold in the blueberries into the bread batter.
- Spread the batter into the greased loaf pan.
- Bake for 60-70 minutes or until an inserted toothpick comes out clean.
- Allow the loaf to cool in the pan for about 30 minutes before taking it out of the pan. Then let the pan cool on a baking rack for at least 60 minutes before adding the icing, refrigerating or freezing.

Keto Lemon Glaze

- To make the lemon glaze imply combine the confectioners sugar substitute, lemon juice, lemon extract, lemon zest and heavy whipping cream. Stir until fully incorporated.

Notes

- Baking times: For a 10X5 inch loaf pan 60-75 minutes. Check for doneness at the 60 minute mark and add foil and bake up to 15 minutes more if necessary.

- For two 6 inch loaf pans check for doneness at 35 minute mark and bake up to 45 minutes if necessary.

Nutrition Info

- Calories: 350
- Total Fat: 30.6g
- Saturated Fat: 11.4g
- Cholesterol: 154mg
- Sodium: 157mg
- Carbohydrates: 7.2g
- Fiber: 3.5g
- Sugar: 2.3g
- Protein: 10.3g

30. Keto Banana Bread

A delicious version of Keto Banana Bread. I may be a little controversial with this recipe but I am providing options to satisfy all keto needs.

Prep Time: 10 minutes
Cook Time: 1 hour
Total Time: 1 hour 5 minutes
Servings: 16 serves

Ingredients

- 80 g butter melted
- 25 g sugar free maple syrup
- 1 cup (150g) Sukrin Gold sweetener or Lakanto Gold sweetener
- 2 teaspoons ground cinnamon
- 1/2 teaspoon nutmeg fresh grated
- 1 teaspoon vanilla
- 100 g banana
- 60 g golden flax meal or golden flax seeds milled extra fine
- 20 g coconut flour
- 150 g almond meal
- 1 tablespoon baking powder I totally recommend Bobs Red Mill Baking Powder for best rise
- 10 g psyllium husk powder or chia flour
- 1 teaspoon xanthan gum
- 4 eggs
- 80 g Greek natural yogurt

OPTIONAL

- 2 teaspoons banana extract INSTEAD of banana
- 1 cup walnuts or brazil nuts chopped

Instructions

- Preheat oven 170?. Line a 22cm x 11cm loaf tine with baking paper.

CONVENTIONAL METHOD

- Over medium heat cook butter, maple syrup, sweetener, cinnamon and nutmeg until butter has melted.
- In a large mixing bowl mash bananas. Pour in melted butter mixture and combine well.
- Add remaining ingredients including nuts (if using) and fold until combined.
- Scoop batter into prepared loaf tin. Smooth over top of loaf with wet spatula.
- Bake 60 minutes or until a skewer comes out clean. Cool 5 minutes in pan before transferring to wire rack to cool completely.

THERMOMIX METHOD

- Add butter, maple syrup, sweetener, cinnamon and nutmeg and cook 5 minutes/100?/stir.
- Add banana and mix 10 seconds speed 4. Scrape sides of bowl
- Add remaining ingredients. Mix 30 seconds/speed 3. Fold though nuts (if using) Follow instructions from Step 4 above.

Nutrition Info
- Calories: 141kcal
- Carbohydrates: 6g
- Protein: 4g
- Fat: 11g
- Saturated Fat: 3g
- Cholesterol: 51mg
- Sodium: 63mg
- Potassium: 150mg
- Fiber: 2g
- Sugar: 1g
- Vitamin A: 3.8%
- Vitamin C: 0.7%
- Calcium: 7.7%
- Iron: 5%

31. Ultimate Dairy-Free Keto Bread

Prep Time 5 minutes
Cook Time 30 minutes
Servings 4

Ingredients

- 2 oz. macadamia butter OR 3.5 T almond butter + 0.5 T oil (2 oz. total)
- 2 large eggs
- 1 large egg white
- 1 oz. coconut flour
- 1/2 tsp. baking powder
- 1/4 tsp. salt
- 1/2 tsp. erythritol
- 1/2 tbsp. psyllium husks powder

Instructions

-
- Preheat the oven to 350°F (180°C). Line a baking pan with a sheet of parchment paper.
- In a small bowl, combine all the dry ingredients, leaving out only the psyllium husks powder. The coconut flour is best sifted.
- Ultimate Keto Bread
- Make macadamia butter if you don't have any. Just pulse the nuts in a bowl of an S-blade food processor (scraping the sides of the bowl once or twice) until you get runny butter.
- Ultimate Keto Bread

- Mix the eggs and the egg white in a medium bowl using an electric mixer. Add the macadamia butter and mix again until well incorporated.
- Ultimate Keto Bread
- Combine the egg mixture and the dry mixture, and mix well. At the very end, add the psyllium husks powder and mix some more. If you find the mixture to be runny, add in another T of coconut flour and mix well.
- Ultimate Keto Bread
- Use your hands or a spoon to form four disks on the baking pan. Wet your hands to make this step less sticky.
- Bake for 30 minutes.

Nutrition Info

170 Calories,
Fat: 13.4 g (of which Saturated: 3.4 g, MUFA's: 9.3 g),
Total Carbs: 7.5 g,
Fiber: 4.9 g,
Net Carbs: 2.6 g,
Protein: 6.5 g

32. Cheesy Garlic Bread Muffins

Gooey melty cheese in a delicious garlicky low carb muffin. It's like garlic bread in a healthier muffin form! Great for breakfast, lunch, or dinner.

Prep Time 20 mins
Cook Time 25 mins
Total Time 45 mins
Servings: 12
Calories: 322 kcal

Ingredients

- 6 tbsp butter melted
- 5 cloves garlic pressed or finely minced, divided
- 1/2 cup sour cream
- 4 large eggs
- 1 tsp salt
- 3 cups almond flour
- 2 tsp baking powder
- 1 cup shredded Cheddar cheese I used Cabot Seriously Sharp
- 1/4 cup chopped parsley
- 4 ounces shredded mozzarella
- Sea salt for sprinkling

Instructions

- Preheat the oven to 325F and grease a standard-size non-stick muffin tin very well. Set the muffin tin on a large rimmed baking sheet (to catch the drips).
- Combine the melted butter and 3 cloves of the garlic. Set aside.
- In a high-powered blender or a food processor, combine the sour cream, eggs, remaining garlic, and salt. Process until well combined. Add the almond flour, baking powder, cheese, and parsley and process again until smooth.
- Divide half of the batter between the prepared muffin cups and use a spoon to make a small well in the center of each.
- Divide the shredded mozzarella between the muffins, pressing into the wells. Drizzle with about 1 tsp of the garlic butter mixture.
- Divide the remaining batter between each muffin cup, make sure to cover the cheese as best you can. Brush the tops with the remaining garlic butter and sprinkle with sea salt.
- Bake 25 minutes or so, until tops are golden brown and just firm to the touch. These will drip a lot of oil as they bake and it may spill over the sides a bit (hence the baking sheet underneath - to save your oven!).
- Remove and let cool 10 minutes before serving. They are fantastic still warm from the oven with the cheese still gooey. They are great cool too and warm up nicely.

Nutrition Info

Calories 322 Calories from Fat 245; Total Fat 27.17g 42%; Saturated Fat 9.34g 47%; Total Carbohydrates 7.44g 2%; Dietary Fiber 3.07g 12%; Protein 12.83g 26%

33. Keto Low Carb Buns with Psyllium Husk

Delicious low carb buns that taste just like multigrain bread!

Prep Time 10 minutes
Cook Time 30 minutes
Total Time 40 minutes
Servings buns

Ingredients

- 4 tbsp boiling water

Dry Ingredients

- 100 g blanched almond flour (about 3/4 cup tightly packed)
- 2 tbsp psyllium husk powder
- 1 tsp baking powder
- 1 tsp black sesame seeds
- 1 tsp white sesame seeds
- 2 tsp sunflower seeds
- 1 tsp black chia seeds
- 1/2 tsp Himalayan salt
- 1/2 tsp garlic powder

Wet Ingredients

- 1 egg
- 2 egg whites
- 1 tbsp apple cider vinegar (or lemon juice, white vinegar)

- 3 tbsp melted refined coconut oil (or butter, lard, shortening, ghee)

Instructions

- Preheat the oven to 180C/350F.
- In a bowl, mix the dry ingredients with a whisk. In a separate bowl, mix the wet ingredients. Pour the wet ingredients into the dry ingredients and mix with a silicone spatula.
- Slowly pour in the boiling water and continue mixing. The dough will be quite thick and expand as it absorbs the water.
- Separate the dough into 5 and form 5 balls with your hands (the batter is pretty sticky). You can spray some olive oil on your hands to make the dough not stick to you.
- Place the balls over parchment paper on a baking tray and bake for 30 minutes. Take out and let cool before serving or you'll burn your fingers! These come out piping hot!

Notes

- You cannot substitute the psyllium husk powder.
- Please don't leave out the boiling water. You need it to activate the psyllium.
- Make sure to use REFINED coconut oil and not the normal extra-virgin kind as you'll get a huge coconut taste.
- If you double the recipe, you may need to add 1-2 tbsp of hot water to the batter.
- All of our ovens are different, so if you find yours to be too moist, just add 5 more minutes in the oven, or cook them at 190C/375F instead for 30 minutes.

Nutrition Info

- Calories 236 Calories from Fat 187
- Total Fat 20.81g 32%
- Saturated Fat 8.37g 42%
- Cholesterol 42mg 14%
- Sodium 41mg 2%
- Total Carbohydrates 8.34g 3%
- Dietary Fiber 5.34g 21%
- Sugars 0.96g
- Protein 7.53g 15%

34. Coconut Flour Mini Cheese Loaves

The perfect little cheesy mini loaf for lunch boxes. Serve warm with butter.

Prep Time 10 mins
Cook Time 15 mins
Total Time 25 mins
Servings: 1

Ingredients

- 113 g butter softened
- 50 g coconut flour
- 1 tsp baking powder
- salt and pepper to taste
- pinch chilli optional
- 8 eggs - medium
- 0.5 spring onion finely sliced
- 100 g grated/shredded cheese
- Coconut Flour Mini Cheese Loaves Toppings
- 1 pepperoni stick sliced
- 2 tbsp pumpkin seeds

Instructions

- Mix the softened butter with the coconut flour, baking powder salt, pepper and chilli (optional) until smooth.
- Add the eggs one at a time. Stir after each egg is added.
- Gently stir through the sliced spring onion and grated/shredded cheese (reserve some to top each loaf).

- Fill each mini loaf tin (or muffin cases).
- I like to top my mini loaves with a few pepperoni stick slices, then cover with some grated/shredded cheese and finally sprinkle a few pumpkin seeds over.
- Bake at 180C/350F for 15 minutes, or until golden.

Nutrition Info

- Calories 170 Calories from Fat 124
- Total Fat 13.8g 21%
- Saturated Fat 8g 40%
- Total Carbohydrates 2.8g 1%
- Dietary Fiber 1.5g 6%
- Sugars 0.6g
- Protein 6.4g 13

35. Low Carb Keto Garlic Breadsticks

These soft, buttery garlic breadsticks taste like the ones served at restaurants, but they are also low carb, keto and gluten free.

Prep Time: 20 minutes
Cook Time: 18 minutes
Total Time: 38 minutes
Servings: 8 breadsticks (total Serving)

Ingredients:

Breadsticks dough

- 1 1/2 cups part skim low moisture shredded mozzarella cheese
- 2 oz full fat cream cheese
- 1 1/3 cups super-fine almond flour*
- 2 tbsp coconut flour
- 1 1/2 tbsp aluminum free baking powder
- 1 tsp garlic powder
- 1/4 tsp onion powder
- 3 large eggs one egg is reserved for egg wash

Garlic Butter Topping

- 2 cloves garlic minced
- 1 tbsp butter
- 1 tbsp olive oil
- 1 1/2 tbsp grated parmesan cheese
- 1 tsp parsley finely chopped

Instructions

- Preheat oven to 350°F. Line a baking sheet with parchment paper.
- In a small bowl, whisk together almond flour, coconut flour, baking powder, garlic powder and onion powder. Set aside.
- Add mozzarella and cream cheese to a large microwave-safe bowl. Cover the cream cheese with mozzarella (this will prevent the cream cheese from overheating and making a mess in your microwave). Melt in the microwave at 30 second intervals. After each 30 seconds, stir cheese until cheese is completely melted and uniform and resembles a dough in appearance (see photo for reference). This should only take around 1 minute total cooking time. Do not try to microwave the full time at once because some of the cheese will overcook. You can also melt the cheeses over the stove in a double boiler.
- Allow cheese dough to cool slightly (only a few minutes) so that it is still warm to the touch but not too hot. If the cheese is too hot it will cook the eggs. But don't let the cheese cool down completely because then it will turn hard and you will not be able to blend it with the other dough ingredients.
- Add cheese, 2 eggs (remember the third egg is for the egg wash finish at the end only), and almond flour mixture into a food processor with dough blade attachment. Pulse on high speed until the dough is uniform. The dough will be quite sticky, which is normal.
- Scoop out dough with a spatula and place onto a large sheet of plastic wrap. Cover the dough in plastic wrap and knead a few times with the dough inside the plastic wrap until you have a uniform dough ball.

- Wrap your pastry board with plastic wrap until the plastic wrap is taut. You should have the plastic wrap running across the bottom of the board so that the weight of the board will help keep the plastic wrap in place. The plastic wrap should keep your dough from sticking to the board. Lightly coat your hands with oil and divide dough into 8 equal parts. Roll each dough into smooth 1 inch thick sticks.
- Add the final egg to a small bowl and whisk. Generously brush the surface of rolls with egg wash.
- Bake rolls for about 15 minutes in the middle rack of your oven, or until breadsticks are just cooked and just starting to brown.
- While breadsticks are baking, make the garlic butter topping. Add garlic, butter and oil in a small saucepan. Bring to low-medium heat and stir until butter is melted and garlic is lightly browned.
- When breadsticks are just done baking but still pale, remove from oven. Quickly brush them generously with the garlic butter topping (You don't want to interrupt the cooking of the breadsticks for too long.) Sprinkle parmesan cheese and parsley over the breadsticks.
- Place breadsticks back into the oven and bake for an additional 3 minutes or until breadsticks turn a golden brown.
- If desired, sprinkle more parmesan cheese and parsley over breadsticks before serving. You can serve breadsticks plain or with low carb marinara sauce.

Nutrition Info

Calories 248 Calories from Fat 180; Total Fat 20g 31%; Saturated Fat 6g 30%; Cholesterol 78mg 26%; Sodium 194mg 8%; Potassium 279mg 8%; Total Carbohydrates 7g 2%; Dietary Fiber 2g 8%; Sugars 1g.

36. Keto Zucchini Bread

A delicious Keto Zucchini Bread that goes perfectly with grass-fed butter - and is a great way to use up all that extra zucchini from the garden!

Prep Time 20 minutes
Cook Time 1 hour
Total Time 1 hour 20 minutes
Serving: 8 servings

Ingredients

- ½ cup butter, softened
- ¼ cup Allulose
- ¼ cup Lakanto Granular Sweetener
- 3 Eggs
- 2 cups Almond Flour
- ½ cup Coconut Flour
- 1 ½ cups Grated Zucchini (approx. 1 medium zucchini)
- 1 tsp. Baking Soda
- 1 tsp. Baking Powder
- 2 tsp. Cinnamon
- 1 tsp. Ginger
- ½ tsp. Xanthan Gum

Instructions

- Preheat oven to 325. Grease a loaf pan with coconut or avocado oil cooking spray and set aside.

- In a large mixing bowl, cream together the butter, allulose, and lakanto sweetener until light and fluffy.
- Add in the eggs, one at a time, beating until combined, then stir in the grated zucchini.
- Dump the almond flour, coconut flour, baking soda, baking powder, cinnamon, ginger, and xanthan gum on top of the wet ingredients, then mix well.
- Scoop the batter into the loaf pan (It will most likely be thick) and spread out evenly.
- Bake at 325 for 50-60 minutes, until set in the center. Remove from the oven and let sit in the loaf pan until completely cool - and be sure to keep an eye on your dog!
- Enjoy with butter, my favorite topping.

Nutrition Info

- Calories: 317
- Total Fat: 28g
- Carbohydrates: 8g
- Fiber: 4g
- Protein: 8g

37. Keto Fiber Bread Rolls Recipe

Perfectly made those Low Carb and Keto Fiber Bread Rolls Recipe are extremely delicious and irresistible to make. One look at them will convince you to try and make them right this moment.

Prep Time 10 minutes
Cook Time 40 minutes
Total Time 50 minutes
Serving: 11 Serving Size: 1

Ingredients

- 150g (1.5 Cups) Almond Flour
- 30g (1/4 Cup) Protein
- 1 Pkt (16g)(4tsp) Baking Powder
- 75g (3/4 Cup)Potato or Oat Fiber
- 15g (3Tbsp)Psyllium Husk
- 250g (1 Cup)Greek Yogurt
- 4 Eggs
- 4 Tbsp (25g) Oil
- 2 Tbsp Water
- 2 Tbsp Vinegar
- 1 tsp salt

Instructions

- Heat up the oven to 150C or 300F
- Mix all of the dry ingredience
- Separate eggs and mix all of the eggwhites first. Set aside

- Mix egg yolks fully.
- Add Yogurt and all of the wet ingredients
- Spoon by spoon keep adding all of the mixed dry ingredients
- At the end add egg whites and mix it gently and fully
- Cover the bowl and let it rest for half hour
- Prepare a baking sheet with Parchment paper
- Once rested, with wet hand make small balls, which you then flatten a bit at the end with hands to achieve rolls
- Once all is on the baking sheet, add a little bit of Potato or Oat Fiber to achieve the white look after baking
- With knife of your super Kaiser Roll Shaper Gadget press on each Roll to give it the perfect end touch
- Place it into the oven and bake for 40 Minutes
- Bon Appetit

Notes

For this recipe you can use Potato Fiber or Oat Fiber to achieve the results, which are identical.

Nutrition Info
- Calories: 177
- Total Fat: 14g
- Carbohydrates: 7g
- Fiber: 7g
- Protein: 11g

38. Almond Flour Bread

An easy recipe for a quick, filling and tasty almond flour bread. This almond flour bread is keto and paleo, and works great with both savory and sweet toppings.

Prep Time10 mins
Cook Time45 mins
Rest time30 mins
Total Time1 hr 25 mins
Servings: 16 slices

Ingredients

- 1 teaspoon coconut oil for pan
- 5 large eggs
- 5 tablespoons refined coconut oil, gently melted in microwave (2.5 oz)
- 1 teaspoon apple cider vinegar (don't skip – helps the bread rise)
- 1/4 teaspoon kosher salt
- 1 3/4 cup almond flour (7 oz)
- 1/2 teaspoon baking soda

Instructions

Preheat oven to 350 degrees F. Grease an 8-inch loaf pan (a 9-inch pan will be too big).

- In a medium bowl, whisk the eggs. Whisk in the coconut oil, vinegar, salt, almond flour and finally the baking soda.

- Pour the batter into the prepared loaf pan.
- Bake until bread is golden-brown and set, and a toothpick inserted in center comes out clean, about 45 minutes.
- Cool 10 minutes in pan on a wire rack before gently releasing the bread from the pan (carefully run a knife along edges if needed). Cool to room temperature, about 20 minutes more, before slicing and serving.
- Keep leftovers in a ziploc bag in the fridge for a few days, or freeze.

Nutrition Info

- Calories 131 Calories from Fat 108
- Total Fat 12g 18%
- Sodium 83mg 3%
- Total Carbohydrates 3g 1%
- Dietary Fiber 1g 4%
- Protein 5g

39. Rosemary Olive Bread

This rosemary olive bread is baked with coconut flour in the shape of a circular loaf. Although the shape is not mandatory, it looks pretty.

Prep Time: 10 minutes
Cook Time: 35 minutes
Total Time: 45 minutes
Servings: 10 Slices

Ingredients

- 1/2 cup Coconut flour
- 4 medium Eggs
- 4 tablespoons Olive oil
- 2 tablespoons Pysllium husk powder
- 1 tablespoon Apple cider vinegar
- 1 tablespoon Baking powder
- 1/2 teaspoon Salt
- 1 1/2 tablespoons Rosemary dried or fresh
- 75 grams Black or green olives chopped
- 1/2 cups Boiling water

Instructions

- Preheat the oven to 180C/350F degrees
- Place the coconut flour, baking powder, rosemary, psyllium husk powder and salt in a bowl and mix thoroughly.
- Add the oil and eggs and blend well until the mixture looks like breadcrumbs.
- Add the apple cider vinegar and mix well.

- Add the chopped olives to the bread and mix.
- Gently add the water, a bit at time and stir into the mixture (you may not need it all).
- Line a baking tray with parchment paper.
- Using your hands, make a large ball of the dough (I find keeping my hands wet helps with the sticky dough).
- Place the dough on the parchment paper lined baking tray.
- Score the top to make a pattern is optional!
- Bake for 35 minutes until golden and firm.
- Eat and enjoy!

Nutrition Info

- Serving: 1 Slice
- Calories: 123kcal
- Carbohydrates: 6g
- Protein: 3g, Fat: 9g

40. Keto Cream Cheese Bread

Keto cream cheese bread is a low carb bread recipe that is made with coconut flour making it keto-friendly as well as nut-free.

Prep Time: 5 minutes
Cook Time: 25 minutes
Additional Time: 5 minutes
Total Time: 35 minutes
Serving: 12

Ingredients

- 8 large eggs
- 8 ounces of full-fat cream cheese (room temperature)
- ½ cup of unsalted butter (room temperature)
- 1 ½ cups coconut flour
- ½ cup of full-fat sour cream
- 4 teaspoons of baking powder
- 1 teaspoon of sea salt
- 1 tablespoon of sugar substitute
- 2 tablespoons of sesame seeds (optional)

Instructions

- Allow your eggs, cream cheese, butter to come to room temperature.
- Pre-heat your oven to 350 degrees.
- Grease a 12 cavity muffin pan generously with butter or a 10 inch loaf pan.

- In a medium-sized bowl combine your coconut flour, baking powder, sea salt, sugar substitute and set aside.
- In a large bowl using a handheld electric mixer or a standup mixer beat together the room temperature butter, cream cheese until light and fluffy. Be sure to scrape the sides of bowl several times to make sure the mixture is well blended.
- To this butter and cream cheese mixture add the 8 eggs one at a time. Making sure to scrape the sides of the bowl several times. Note that due to the large number of eggs the mixture will not fully combine, this is normal. Once you add the dry ingredients to this wet mixture, the ingredients will come together perfectly.
- To the wet ingredients slowly add all the dry ingredients on a low mixing setting. Making sure to scrape the bowl a couple of times.
- Once the two mixtures are fully combined stop using the electric mixture and fold in the 1/2 cup of sour cream gently. Making sure the sour cream gets fully incorporated into the batter but being careful to not over mix.Note that the batter will be very thick and fluffy. This is the normal texture when using coconut flour exclusively in a recipe.
- Overfill the muffin pan just slightly. The thick batter will not cause the muffins to spread. Slightly overfilling your muffin tins will create a nice muffin top.
- With one additional whole egg and a tablespoon of water create an egg wash. Baste the top of each muffin with the egg wash and then sprinkle the sesame seeds on top of each muffin. This step is optional.
- Bake the muffins for 25-30 minutes until lightly brown on the top and when an inserted toothpick comes out clean.
- Report this ad

- If you are baking your keto cream cheese bread in a 10 inch loaf, bake the bread for up to 90 minutes. Check your bread at 60 minutes for doneness and allow to cook longer if necessary.

Nutrition Info

- Calories: 204
- Total Fat: 19.4g
- Saturated Fat: 11.4g
- Cholesterol: 154mg
- Sodium: 160mg
- Carbohydrates: 2.2g
- Fiber: 0.6g
- Sugar: 0.4g
- Protein: 5.8g

41. Cheddar Garlic Fathead Rolls

These keto dinner rolls are melt-in-your-mouth delicious. Made with cheddar cheese fathead dough, they are the perfect low carb side dish for all of your favorite meals. They make great sandwiches too.

Prep Time 10 mins
Cook Time 25 mins
Total Time 35 mins
Servings: 8 servings

Ingredients

Rolls:

- 8 ounces cheddar cheese grated (I used Cabot Vermont Cheddar)
- 2 tbsp butter
- 1/2 cup coconut flour
- 1/4 cup unflavored whey protein powder or egg white protein powder
- 4 tsp baking powder
- 1 tsp garlic powder
- 1/4 tsp salt
- 2 large eggs
- 1 large egg white

Garlic Butter

- 2 tbsp butter melted
- 2 cloves garlic minced

- 1 tbsp chopped parsley
- 1/2 tsp coarse salt

Instructions

- Preheat the oven to 350F and line an 8-inch round baking pan with parchment paper.
- In a large microwave safe bowl, combine the grated cheese and the butter. Melt on high in 30 second increments until the cheese and butter can be stirred together and is almost liquid.
- Add the coconut flour, protein powder, baking powder, garlic powder, and salt. Stir in the eggs and egg white and use a rubber spatula to "knead" together in the bowl until uniform.
- Divide the dough into 8 equal portions. The dough will be quite sticky so lightly oil your hands and roll into 8 ball. Place in the prepared baking pan.
- Whisk together the ingredients for the garlic butter and brush about half of it over the rolls in the pan.
- Bake 20 to 25 minutes, until puffed, golden brown, and firm to the touch. Remove and let cool about15 minutes before removing from the pan and breaking apart. Brush with the remaining garlic butter. Serve warm.

Nutrition Info

- Calories 230 Calories from Fat 143
- Total Fat 15.9g 24%
- Total Carbohydrates 5.9g 2%
- Dietary Fiber 2.6g 10%
- Protein 12.2g 24%

42. Coconut Flour Pizza Crust

This coconut flour pizza crust is the best gluten-free pizza crust I've ever tried. It's soft and tasty, and sturdy enough to hold with your hands!

Prep Time 10 mins
Cook Time 20 mins
Total Time 30 mins
Servings: 2 (8-inch) pizzas

Ingredients

- Olive oil spray for pans
- 4 large eggs
- 2 tablespoons water
- 1 teaspoon garlic powder
- 1 teaspoon onion powder
- 1 teaspoon dried oregano
- 1/4 cup coconut flour
- 6 tablespoons grated parmesan cheese (1 oz)

Topping:

- 1/2 cup marinara sauce
- 1 cup shredded part-skim mozzarella (4 oz)

Instructions

- Preheat oven to 400 degrees F.

- Line two pizza pans with parchment paper and spray the paper with olive oil. You can also make these pizzas side by side on a single, large baking sheet.
- In a large bowl, whisk the eggs with the water, garlic powder, onion powder and dried oregano.
- Measure out the coconut flour, breaking up any lumps with your hands. Stir the coconut flour into the egg mixture, mixing until smooth.
- Stir in the Parmesan cheese.
- Allow the mixture to rest and thicken for a couple of minutes. This will allow the coconut flour to soak up the liquid.
- Using a rubber spatula, transfer half of the mixture onto each of the prepared pans. Use a spatula to spread it out evenly into an 8-inch circle.
- Bake the pizzas until set and the edges are beginning to brown, about 15 minutes. The crust will still be light at this point, and that's OK.
- Remove the pizzas from the oven and switch the oven to broil. Position the top oven rack 6 inches below flame.
- Spread each pizza with half the pizza sauce, sprinkle with half the shredded mozzarella, and add any other toppings you like (I used Applegate's pepperoni).
- Broil each pizza until cheese is melted and crust is golden-brown, 2-3 minutes.

Nutrition Info

Calories 496 Calories from Fat 297; Total Fat 33g 51%; Saturated Fat 15g 75%; Sodium 885mg 37%; Total Carbohydrates 13g 4%; Dietary Fiber 5g 20%; Sugars 14g; Protein 35g 70%

43. Low Carb Blueberry English Muffin Bread Loaf

Prep Time 15 minutes
Cook Time 45 minutes
Total Time 1 hour
Servings 12

Ingredients

- 1/2 cup almond butter or cashew or peanut butter
- 1/4 cup butter ghee or coconut oil
- 1/2 cup almond flour
- 1/2 tsp salt
- 2 tsp baking powder
- 1/2 cup almond milk unsweetened
- 5 eggs beaten
- 1/2 cup blueberries

Instructions

- Preheat oven to 350 degrees F.
- In a microwavable bowl melt nut butter and butter together for 30 seconds, stir until combined well.
- In a large bowl, whisk almond flour, salt and baking powder together. Pour the nut butter mixture into the large bowl and stir to combine.
- Whisk the almond milk and eggs together then pour into the bowl and stir well.
- Drop in fresh blueberries or break apart frozen blueberries and gently stir into the batter.

- Line a loaf pan with parchment paper and lightly grease the parchment paper as well.
- Pour the batter into the loaf pan and bake 45 minutes or until a toothpick in center comes out clean.
- Cool for about 30 minutes then remove from pan.
- Slice and toast each slice before serving.

Recipe Notes

Net Carbs: 3g

44. Keto Pumpkin Bread

A delicious, moist, keto pumpkin bread full of warm spices and amazing pumpkin flavor. Made with almond and coconut flours to keep it healthy, gluten-free, and low-carb.

Prep Time: 10 minutes
Cook Time: 45 minutes
Total Time: 55 minutes
Serving: 10

Ingredients

- 1/2 cup butter, softened
- 2/3 cup erythritol sweetener, like Swerve
- 4 eggs large
- 3/4 cup pumpkin puree, canned (see notes for fresh)
- 1 tsp vanilla extract
- 1 1/2 cup almond flour
- 1/2 cup coconut flour
- 4 tsp baking powder
- 1 tsp cinnamon
- 1/2 tsp nutmeg
- 1/4 tsp ginger
- 1/8 tsp cloves
- 1/2 tsp salt

Instructions

- Preheat the oven to 350°F. Grease a 9"x5" loaf pan, and line with parchment paper.
- In a large mixing bowl, cream the butter and sweetener together until light and fluffy.
- Add the eggs, one at a time, and mix well to combine.
- Add the pumpkin puree and vanilla, and mix well to combine.
- In a separate bowl, stir together the almond flour, coconut flour, baking powder, cinnamon, nutmeg, ginger, cloves, salt. Break up any lumps of almond flour or coconut flour.
- Add the dry ingredients to the wet ingredients, and stir to combine. (Optionally, add up to 1/2 cup of mix-ins, like chopped nuts or chocolate chips.)
- Pour the batter into the prepared loaf pan. Bake for 45 - 55 minutes, or until a toothpick inserted into the center of the loaf comes out clean.
- If the bread is browning too quickly, you can cover the pan with a piece of aluminum foil.

Notes

- Want to use your own homemade puréed pumpkin? If it's thinner than canned pumpkin, try to remove some of the water to prevent soggy pumpkin bread.
- Want cream cheese frosting? Check the post above for an easy cream cheese frosting recipe.
- Want some nuts or chocolate chips? Feel free to add 1/2 cup of mix-ins to the batter before baking
- Want pumpkin muffins instead? Divide the batter into greased muffin tins. Be sure to reduce the baking time.

Nutrition Info
- Calories: 165
- Total Fat: 14g
- Saturated Fat: 7g
- Unsaturated Fat: 4g
- Cholesterol: 99mg
- Sodium: 76mg
- Carbohydrates: 6g
- Fiber: 3g
- Sugar: 1g
- Protein: 5g

45. Cranberry Jalapeño "Cornbread" Muffins

Low carb, grain-free muffins that taste like cornbread! Made with coconut flour and bursting with cranberries and jalapeño, these delicious muffins would make a great addition to any Thanksgiving table.

Prep Time 10 mins
Cook Time 30 mins
Total Time 40 mins
Servings: 12 muffins
Calories: 157 kcal

Ingredients

- 1 cup coconut flour (I used Bob's Red Mill)
- 1/3 cup Swerve Sweetener or other erythritol
- 1 tbsp baking powder
- 1/2 tsp salt
- 7 large eggs, lightly beaten
- 1 cup unsweetened almond milk
- 1/2 cup butter, melted OR avocado oil
- 1/2 tsp vanilla
- 1 cup fresh cranberries, cut in half
- 3 tbsp minced jalapeño peppers
- 1 jalapeño, seeds removed, sliced into 12 slices, for garnish

Instructions

- Preheat oven to 325F and grease a muffin tin well or line with paper liners.

- In a medium bowl, whisk together coconut flour, sweetener, baking powder and salt. Break up any clumps with the back of a fork.
- Stir in eggs, melted butter and almond milk and stir vigorously. Stir in vanilla extract and continue to stir until mixture is smooth and well combined. Stir in chopped cranberries and jalapeños.
- Divide batter evenly among prepared muffin cups and place one slice of jalapeño on top of each.
- Bake 25 to 30 minutes or until tops are set and a tester inserted in the center comes out clean. Let cool 10 minutes in pan, then transfer to a wire rack to cool completely.

Nutrition Info
- Calories 157 Calories from Fat 101
- Total Fat 11.22g 17%
- Saturated Fat 7.11g 36%
- Cholesterol 128mg 43%
- Sodium 362mg 15%
- Total Carbohydrates 7.08g 2%
- Dietary Fiber 3.84g 15%
- Protein 5.21g 10%

46. 3 Minute Low Carb Biscuits

Prep Time: 2 minutes
Cook Time: 3 minutes
Total Time: 5 minutes
Servings: 1 Servings
Calories: 392kcal

Ingredients

- 1 tbsp Butter
- 2 tbsp Coconut flour
- 1 large Egg
- 1 tbsp Heavy Whipping Cream
- 2 tbsp Water
- 1/4 cup Cheddar Cheese
- 1/8 tsp garlic powder
- 1/8 tsp Onion powder
- 1/8 tsp Dried Parsley
- 1/8 tsp Pink Himalayan Salt
- 1/8 tsp black pepper
- 1/4 tsp Baking powder

Instructions

- Melt butter in a coffee mug by microwaving for 20 seconds.
- Add coconut flour, baking powder, and seasonings. Mix to incorporate with a fork.
- Add egg, water, cheese and heavy whipping cream. Mix until combined.

- Microwave for 3 minutes. Immediately remove from mug and allow to cool for 2 minutes.
- Slice and enjoy.

Nutrition Info

- Calories: 392kcal
- Carbohydrates: 9g
- Protein: 15g
- Fat: 32g
- Fiber: 5g

47. Coconut flour flatbread

Coconut flour flatbread Ketogenic flatbread perfect as a side to curries or a low carb tortillas wraps. 100% Vegan + eggless + gluten free soft breads.

Prep Time10 mins
Cook Time5 mins
Total Time15 mins
Servings: 6 flatbreads

Ingredients

- 2 tablespoons psyllium husk (9g)
- 1/2 cup coconut flour fine, fresh, no lumps (60g)
- 1 cup lukewarm water (240ml)
- 1 tablespoon olive oil (15ml)
- 1/4 teaspoons baking soda

- 1/4 teaspoons salt - optional

Cooking

- 1 teaspoon olive oil to rub/oil the non stick pan

Instructions

Make the dough

- In a medium mixing bowl, combine the psyllium husk and coconut flour (if lumps are in your flour use a fork to smash them BEFORE measuring the flour, amount must be precise).
- Add in the lukewarm water (I used tap water about 40C/bath temperature), olive oil, and baking soda. Give a good stir with a spatula, then use your hands to knead the dough. Add salt now if you want. I never add the salt in contact with baking soda to avoid deactivating the leaving agent.
- Knead for 1 minute. The dough is moist and it gets softer and slightly dryer as you go. It should come together easily to form a dough as on my picture. If not, too sticky, add more husk, 1/2 teaspoon at a time, knead for 30 sec and see how it goes. The dough will always be a bit moist but it shouldn't stick to your hands at all. It must come together as a dough.
- Set aside 10 minute in the mixing bowl.
- Now the dough must be soft, elastic and hold well together, it is ready to roll.
- Roll/ shape the flatbread
- Cut the dough into 4 even pieces, roll each pieces into a small ball.
- Place one of the dough ball between two pieces of parchment paper, press the ball with your hand palm to stick it well to the paper and start rolling with a rolling pin as thin as you like

a bread. My breads are 20 cm diameter (8 inches) and I made 6 flatbread with this recipe.
- Un peel the first layer of parchment paper from your flatbread. Use a lid to cut out round flatbread. Keep the outside dough to reform a ball and roll more flatbread - that is how I make 2 extra flatbread from the 4 balls above!

Cook in non stick pan

- Warm a non stick tefal crepe/ pancake pan under medium/high heat- or use any non stick pan of your choice, the one you would use for your pancakes.
- Add one teaspoon of olive oil or vegetable oil of your choice onto a piece of absorbent paper. Rub the surface of the pan to make sure it is slightly oiled. Don't leave any drops of oil or the bread will fry!
- Flip over the flatbread on the hot pan and peel off carefully the last piece of parchment paper.
- Cook for 2-3 minutes on the first side, flip over using a spatula and cook for 1-2 more minute on the other side.
- Cool down the flatbread on a plate and use as a sandwich wrap later or enjoy hot as a side dish. I recommend a drizzle of olive oil, crushed garlic and herbs before serving ! (optional but delish!)
- Repeat the rolling, cooking for the next 3 flatbread. Make sure you rub the oiled absorbent paper onto the saucepan each time to avoid the bread to stick to the pan.
- Store in the pantry in an airtight box or on a plate covered with plastic wrap to keep them soft, for up to 3 days.

- Rewarm in the same pan or if you want to give them a little crisp rewarm in the hot oven on a baking sheet for 1-2 minutes at 150C.

Nutrition Info

Serving: 1flatbread; Calories: 66kcal; Carbohydrates: 7.3g; Protein: 2g; Fat: 3.3g; Fiber: 4.7g; Sugar: 2g

48. Easy Paleo Keto Bread Recipe - 5 Ingredients

If you want to know how to make the BEST keto bread recipe, this is it! It makes fluffy white paleo bread that's quick & easy. Just 5 basic ingredients!

Course Breakfast, Main Course, Side Dish

Prep Time 10 minutes
Cook Time 1 hour 10 minutes
Total Time 1 hour 20 minutes

Ingredients

Basic Ingredients

- 1 cup Blanched almond flour
- 1/4 cup Coconut flour
- 2 tsp Gluten-free baking powder
- 1/4 tsp Sea salt
- 1/3 cup Butter (or 5 tbsp + 1 tsp; measured solid, then melted; can use coconut oil for dairy-free)
- 12 large Egg white (~1 1/2 cups, at room temperature)

Optional Ingredients (recommended)

- 1 1/2 tbsp Erythritol (can use any sweetener or omit)
- 1/4 tsp Xanthan gum (for texture - omit for paleo)
- 1/4 tsp Cream of tartar (to more easily whip egg whites)

Instructions

- Preheat the oven to 325 degrees F (163 degrees C). Line an 8 1/2 x 4 1/2 in (22x11 cm) loaf pan with parchment paper, with extra hanging over the sides for easy removal later.
- Combine the almond flour, coconut flour, baking powder, erythritol, xanthan gum, and sea salt in a large food processor. Pulse until combined.
- Add the melted butter. Pulse, scraping down the sides as needed, until crumbly.
- In a very large bowl, use a hand mixer to beat the egg whites and cream of tartar (if using), until stiff peaks form. Make sure the bowl is large enough because the whites will expand a lot.
- Add 1/2 of the stiff egg whites to the food processor. Pulse a few times until just combined. Do not over-mix!
- Carefully transfer the mixture from the food processor into the bowl with the egg whites, and gently fold until no streaks remain. Do not stir. Fold gently to keep the mixture as fluffy as possible.
- Transfer the batter to the lined loaf pan and smooth the top. Push the batter toward the center a bit to round the top.
- Bake for about 40 minutes, until the top is golden brown. Tent the top with aluminum foil and bake for another 30-45 minutes, until the top is firm and does not make a squishy sound when

pressed. Internal temperature should be 200 degrees. Cool completely before removing from the pan and slicing.

Nutrition Info
- Calories 82
- Fat 7g
- Protein 4g
- Total Carbs 3g
- Net Carbs 1g
- Fiber 2g
- Sugar 1g

49. Coconut Bread

Prep/Cook Time: 60 mins

Ingredients

- 1/2 cup coconut flour
- 1/4 tsp salt
- 1/4 tsp baking soda
- 6 eggs
- ¼ cup coconut oil, melted
- ¼ unsweetened almond milk

Instructions

- Preheat oven to 350°F.
- Line an 8×4 inch loaf pan with parchment paper.
- In a bowl combine the coconut flour, baking soda and salt.
- In another bowl combine the eggs, milk and oil.
- Slowly add the wet ingredients into the dry ingredients and mix until combined.
- Pour the mixture into the prepared loaf pan.
- Bake for 40-50 minutes, or until a toothpick, inserted in the middle comes out clean.

Nutrition Info

Calories 108; Carbohydrates 3.4 g; Fat 8.7 g; Sugar 0.5 g; Protein 4.2 g; Fiber 2.1 g; Potassium 35.8 mg; Folic Acid (B9) 12.1 µg; Sodium 86 mg

50. Collagen Keto Bread

Prep/Cook Time: 1 hour and 50 minutes (10 minutes active)

Ingredients:

- 1/2 cup Unflavored Grass-Fed Collagen Protein
- 6 tablespoons almond flour (see recipe notes below for nut-free substitute)
- 5 pastured eggs, separated
- 1 tablespoon unflavored liquid coconut oil
- 1 teaspoon aluminum-free baking powder
- 1 teaspoon xanthan gum (see recipe notes for substitute)
- Pinch Himalayan pink salt
- Optional: pinch of stevia

Instructions:

Preheat oven to 325 degrees F.

- Generously oil only the bottom part of a standard size (1.5 quart) glass or ceramic loaf dish with coconut oil (or butter or ghee). Or you may use a piece of parchment paper trimmed to fit the bottom of your dish. Not oiling or lining the sides of your dish will allow the bread to attach to the sides and stay lifted while it cools.

- In a large bowl, beat the egg whites until stiff peaks form. Set aside.
- In a small bowl, whisk the dry ingredients together and set aside. Add the optional pinch of stevia if you're not a fan of eggs. It'll help offset the flavor without adding sweetness to your loaf.

- In a small bowl, whisk together the wet ingredients — egg yolks and liquid coconut oil — and set aside.
- Add the dry and the wet ingredients to the egg whites and mix until well incorporated. Your batter will be thick and a little gooey.
- Pour the batter into the oiled or lined dish and place in the oven.
- Bake for 40 minutes. The bread will rise significantly in the oven.
- Remove from oven and let it cool completely — about 1 to 2 hours. The bread will sink some and that's OK.
- Once the bread is cooled, run the sharp edge of a knife around the edges of the dish to release the loaf.
- Slice into 12 even slices.

Nutrition Info

- Calories: 77
- Protein: 7g
- Carbs: 1g
- Fiber: 1g
- Sugar: 0g

51. Keto Breakfast Pizza

Prep/Cook Time: 25 minutes

Ingredients:

- 2 cups grated cauliflower
- 2 tablespoons coconut flour
- 1/2 teaspoon salt
- 4 eggs
- 1 tablespoon psyllium husk powder (Use a mold-free brand like this one)
- Toppings: smoked Salmon, avocado, herbs, spinach, olive oil (see post for more suggestions)

Instructions:

- Preheat the oven to 350 degrees. Line a pizza tray or sheet pan with parchment.
- In a mixing bowl, add all ingredients except toppings and mix until combined. Set aside for 5 minutes to allow coconut flour and psyllium husk to absorb liquid and thicken up.
- Carefully pour the breakfast pizza base onto the pan. Use your hands to mold it into a round, even pizza crust.
- Bake for 15 minutes, or until golden brown and fully cooked.
- Remove from the oven and top breakfast pizza with your chosen toppings. Serve warm.

Nutrition Info

Calories: 454; Total Fat: 31g; Saturated Fat: 75g; Cholesterol: 348mg; Total Carbs: 26g; Fiber: 17.2g; Sugars: 4.4g; Net Carbs: 8.8g; Protein: 22g

52. Paleo Chocolate Zucchini Bread

Paleo Chocolate Zucchini Bread. Easy, Healthy Gluten free loaf, super moist with almond meal and unsweetened cocoa powder. 100% KETO + Low carb + sugar free

Prep Time 10 mins
Cook Time 50 mins
Cool down 4 hrs
Total Time 1 hr
Servings: 12 slices
Calories: 185kcal

Ingredients

Dry ingredients

- 1 1/2 cup almond flour (170g)
- 1/4 cup unsweetened cocoa powder (25g)
- 1 1/2 teaspoon baking soda
- 2 teaspoons ground cinnamon
- 1/4 teaspoon sea salt
- 1/2 cup sugar free crystal sweetener (Monk fruit or erythritol) (100g) or coconut sugar if refined sugar free

Wet ingredients

- 1 cup zucchini, finely grated measure packed, discard juice/liquid if there is some - about 2 small zucchini
- 1 large egg
- 1/4 cup + 2 tablespoon canned coconut cream 100ml

- 1/4 cup extra virgin coconut oil , melted, 60ml
- 1 teaspoon vanilla extract
- 1 teaspoon apple cider vinegar

Filling - optional

- 1/2 cup sugar free chocolate chips
- 1/2 cup chopped walnuts or nuts you like

Instructions

- Preheat oven to 180C (375F). Line a baking loaf pan (9 inches x 5 inches) with parchment paper. Set aside.
- Remove both extremity of the zucchinis, keep skin on.
- Finely grate the zucchini using a vegetable grater. Measure the amount needed in a measurement cup. Make sure you press/pack them firmly for a precise measure and to squeeze out any liquid from the grated zucchini, I usually don't have any!. If you do, discard the liquid or keep for another recipe.
- In a large mixing bowl, stir all the dry ingredients together: almond flour, unsweetened cocoa powder, sugar free crystal sweetener, cinnamon, sea salt and baking soda. Set aside.
- Add all the wet ingredients into the dry ingredients : grated zucchini, coconut oil, coconut cream, vanilla, egg, apple cider vinegar.
- Stir to combine all the ingredients together.
- Stir in the chopped nuts and sugar free chocolate chips.
- Transfer the chocolate bread batter into the prepared loaf pan.
- Bake 50 - 55 minutes, you may want to cover the bread loaf with a piece of foil after 40 minute to avoid the top to darken too much, up to you.

- The bread will stay slightly moist in the middle and firm up after fully cool down.

Cool down

- Cool down 10 minutes in the loaf pan, then cool down on a cooling rack until it reach room temperature. It can take 4 hours as it is a thick bread. Don' slice the bread before it reach room temperature. If too hot in the center, it will be too oft and fall apart when you slice. For a faster result, cool down 40 minutes at room temperature then pop in the fridge for 1 hour. The fridge will create an extra fudgy texture and the bread will be even easier to slice as it firms up.
- Store in the fridge up to 4 days in a cake bow or airtight container.

Nutrition Info

- Calories: 185kcal
- Carbohydrates: 6.1g
- Protein: 4.9g
- Fat: 17.1g
- Fiber: 2.7g
- Sugar: 1.2g

53. Low-Carb Focaccia Bread with Thyme and Onion

This delicious Low-Carb Focaccia Bread recipe is easy to make, and tastes so rich and wonderful with the addition of thyme and onion.

Prep Time 15minutes
Cook Time 30minutes
Servings 1loaf

Ingredients

- 1/2 cup coconut flour
- 5 tablespoons psyllium husk powder
- 2 teaspoons baking powder
- 1 teapsoon salt
- 4 whole egg
- 1 cup boiling water
- 1 teaspoon dried thyme
- 1 small onions

Instructions

- Add coconut flour, psyllium husk, baking powder and salt in a mixing bowl and combine.
- Mix in the eggs. Work quickly, stirring until the powders firm up into a thick dough.
- Add a cup of boiling water and mix thoroughly.
- Line a baking sheet with parchment paper. Form dough into a flat oval on top of the paper. Use a sharp knife to score diagonal cut through the dough. Sprinkle the top with thyme and additional salt. Thinly slice the onion into rings and arrange

evenly over the thyme and salt. Press gently into the dough to stick.
- Bake at 350 degrees F for 25-30 minutes. The dough rises about twice as high, with a firm crust once done. If the bread feels spongy to the touch, continue cooking.`
- Remove from the oven and cool slightly before cutting; serve warm or cold. Store in the fridge.

Recipe Notes

Marcos per serving: 3.0 g fat, 9.0 g carb, 2.6 g net carb, 3.7 g protein

Nutrition Info

Calories per slice: 79.5 total calories

54. Cheesy Skillet Bread

Easy low carb skillet bread with a wonderful crust of cheddar cheese. This keto bread recipe is perfect with soups and stews.

Prep Time 10 mins
Cook Time 16 mins
Total Time 26 mins
Servings: 10

Ingredients

- 1 tbsp butter for the skillet
- 2 cups almond flour
- 1/2 cup flax seed meal

- 2 tsp baking powder
- 1/2 tsp salt
- 1 & 1/2 cups shredded Cheddar cheese divided
- 3 large eggs lightly beaen
- 1/2 cup butter melted
- 3/4 cup almond milk

Instructions

- Preheat oven to 425F. Add 1 tbsp butter to a 10-inch oven-proof skillet and place in oven.
- In a large bowl, whisk together almond flour, flax seed meal, baking powder, salt and 1 cup of the shredded cheddar cheese.
- Stir in the eggs, melted butter and almond milk until thoroughly combined.
- Remove hot skillet from oven (remember to put on your oven mitts), and swirl butter to coat sides.
- Pour batter into pan and smooth the top. Sprinkle with remaining 1/2 cup cheddar.
- Bake 16 to 20 minutes, or until browned around the edges and set through the middle. Cheese on top should be nicely browned.
- Remove and let cool 15 minutes.

Recipe Notes

Serves 10. Each serving has 7.2 g of carbs and 4 g of fiber. Total NET CARBS = 3.2 g.

Nutrition Info

- Calories 357 Calories from Fat 276
- Total Fat 30.63g 47%
- Total Carbohydrates 7.9g 3%
- Dietary Fiber 4.77g 19%
- Protein 12.48g 25%

55. Keto Flax Seed Bread

Prep Time 5 minutes
Cook Time 2 minutes
Total Time 7 minutes
Servings 2 Slices

Ingredients

- 1 tablespoon Softened Butter
- 4 tablespoons Organic Ground Flaxseed Meal
- 1 Large Egg
- ½ teaspoon Baking Powder
- ½ teaspoon Salt

Instructions

- Grab your Pyrex glass square dish and add the butter. Melt it in the microwave for a few seconds.
- Crack your egg into the dish and give it a good mix with a fork.
- Mix the ground flax seed, salt and baking powder in a separate bowl and combine.

- Add all the mixed dry ingredients, ground flax, salt, and baking powder directly into the baking dish and combine all ingredients thoroughly.
- It will turn into a thick texture. Flatten out the surface of the mixture to ensure even cooking.
- Cook in the microwave for two minutes.
- Leave to cool for a few minutes before taking out.
- Use a spatula and gently pull the bread away from the side of the dish. After you turn it upside down, it should come out without difficulty.
- Grab your bread knife and cut it in half to make two slices

56. Keto Mini Bread Loaves

Prep/Cook Time: 1 hour 10 mins
Serving: 32

Ingredients

2 cups almond flour

- 1/2 cup psyllium husk powder
- 1/2 cup ground flax
- 4 teaspoons baking powder
- 2 tablespoons coconut flour
- 2 teaspoons Pink Himalayan sea salt
- 5 teaspoons Apple Cider Vinegar
- 1 3/4 cups boiling water
- 4 egg whites
- 2 eggs

Instructions

- Preheat oven to 350 degrees.
- Mix the almond flour, coconut flour, psyllium husk, flax, sea salt, and baking powder in a medium bowl.
- Meanwhile, boil the water.
- In a small bowl beat the eggs whites, eggs and vinegar lightly (just quick enough to combine it all).
- Add the eggs and vinegar mixture into the bowl with the dry ingredients. Mix with a hand whisk for about 20-30 seconds.
- Add the hot water and whisk for another 30 seconds. Then use your hand (be careful, it will still be hot) and mix for another 10 seconds using a folding motion. The dough will get more "doughy" as you do this.
- Since your hands will already be goopy, just scoop it equally into the 4 mini loaf molds.
- Smooth out the top a bit, but it doesn't need to be perfect.
- Bake for 50-55 minutes and remove from oven.
- While they are still hot, remove from loaf pan. You can use a knife or thin spatula to separate the sides and then pop it out.
- Let cool on a wire rack.

Nutrition Info

- Calories 73.28
- Total Fat 4.38g
- Saturated Fat 0.45g
- Sodium 78.76mg
- Carbohydrates 6.78g
- Fiber 4.77g
- Sugar 0.31g

57. Low Carb Asparagus Egg Bites

These Asparagus Egg Bites make the perfect snack - especially on the go! Low carb, keto, and gluten free recipe.

Prep Time: 5 minutes
Cook Time: 15 minutes
Total Time: 20 minutes
Servings: 3

Ingredients

- non-stick cooking spray
- 3 medium asparagus stalks
- 6 eggs
- 1 tbs unsweetened almond milk
- salt and pepper
- 2 tbs grated Parmesan

Instructions

- Preheat the oven to 400F (200C).
- Prepare a six-hole muffin pan by spraying it liberally with some non-stick cooking spray. Chop up the asparagus (to make about half a cup) and divide between the muffin pan cups.
- Beat the eggs and unsweetened almond milk together in a jug. Season with salt and pepper then divide it between the muffin cups.
- Sprinkle some grated Parmesan over the top of each one, then bake in a preheated oven for 12-15 minutes, until golden brown

on top and the egg is cooked through. They will puff up while cooking but deflate slightly as they cool.
- Remove the asparagus egg bites from the pan and enjoy warm - or let cool fully and store in the fridge.

Nutrition Info

- Calories 143 Calories from Fat 81
- Total Fat 9g 14%
- Saturated Fat 3g 15%
- Trans Fat 0g
- Sodium 178mg 7%
- Potassium 153mg 4%
- Total Carbohydrates 1g 0%
- Dietary Fiber 0g 0%
- Sugars 0g
- Protein 12g 24%

58. Cheesy Low Carb Biscuits

Easy and delicious low carb biscuits recipe made with Cheddar cheese and sour cream. Perfect with soup, or as a breakfast biscuit. They even make great sandwiches.

Prep Time 10 mins
Cook Time 25 mins
Total Time 35 mins
Servings: 10 biscuits

Ingredients

- 1/2 cup coconut flour
- 1/2 cup almond flour
- 2 tsp baking powder
- 1 tsp garlic powder
- 1/2 tsp salt
- 3/4 cup shredded Cheddar cheese divided (I recommend Cabot Private Stock)
- 4 large eggs OR 3 large egg whites and 2 large eggs
- 3/4 cup sour cream or Greek yogurt I recommend Cabot full fat sour cream
- 1/4 cup butter melted

Instructions

- Preheat oven to 350F and line a large baking sheet with parchment or a silicone mat.

- In a large bowl, whisk together the coconut flour, almond flour, baking powder, garlic powder and salt. Whisk in 1/2 cup of the shredded Cheddar.
- Stir in eggs, sour cream and melted butter until well combined.
- Drop by rounded spoonfuls onto prepared baking sheet. These are very filling and they spread and rise so make the mounds smallish. You should get 10 to 12 biscuits.
- Sprinkle with remaining 1/4 cup Cheddar.
- Bake 20 to 23 minutes, until firm to the touch and cheese is just starting to brown.
- Remove and let cool 5 minutes.

Nutrition Info

- Calories 185 Calories from Fat 128
- Total Fat 14.2g 22%
- Total Carbohydrates 5.6g 2%
- Dietary Fiber 2.6g 10%
- Protein 6.8g 14%

59. Grain Free Irish Soda Bread (Low Carb and Sugar-Free)

Prep Time 15 minutes
Cook Time 40 minutes
Total Time 55 minutes
Servings 12 servings

Ingredients

- 2 cups sunflower seeds
- 1/2 cup ground flaxseed
- 2 tablespoons coconut flour
- 1/4 cup Swerve sweetener
- 2 teaspoon baking powder
- 1/2 teaspoon salt
- 2 tablespoons butter cold unsalted
- 2 eggs
- 1/4 cup coconut milk
- 1/4 cup raisins or currants

Instructions

- Preheat oven to 350 degrees.
- Grind the sunflower seeds in a food processor.
- Add the flaxseed, coconut flour, swerve, baking powder (or soda) and salt.
- Pulse in the butter.
- Add remaining ingredients, except raisins.
- Remove dough and transfer to a bowl.
- Mix in raisins or currants.

- Wet hands to form shape and place in a greased cast iron skillet.
- Score an x in the middle and bake 30 minutes.
- Reduce the temperature to 325 and bake another 5-10 minutes or until golden on top.
- Allow to cool before slicing.

Recipe Notes

Net Carbs: 6g

60. Low Carb Carrot Cake Muffins

This low carb carrot cake muffins are great for snacking! Sugar free, gluten free, and keto recipe.

Prep Time: 10 minutes
Cook Time: 25 minutes
Cooling Time: 5 minutes
Total Time: 35 minutes
Servings: 6

Ingredients

- 1 carrot peeled and grated
- 1 cup almond flour
- 3 eggs
- ¼ cup melted butter
- 2 tbs low carb sweetener eg Swerve
- ½ tsp baking powder
- ½ tsp vanilla extract

Instructions

- Preheat the oven to 350F (175C).
- In a stand mixer bowl, add almond flour, eggs, melted butter, sweetener, baking powder and vanilla extract. Blend until fully combined.
- Stir in the grated carrot until mixed through the batter.
- Divide the mixture between a six-hole muffin pan that has been lined with paper or silicone liners.
- Bake in a preheated oven for 20-25 minutes or until cooked through. Let cool for 5 minutes before serving.

Nutrition Info

- Calories 210 Calories from Fat 171
- Total Fat 19g 29%
- Saturated Fat 6g 30%
- Cholesterol 102mg 34%
- Sodium 105mg 4%
- Potassium 102mg 3%
- Total Carbohydrates 5g 2%
- Dietary Fiber 2g 8%
- Sugars 1g
- Protein 6g 12%

61. Sweet Keto Challah Bread Recipe

Sweet Keto Challah Bread Recipe (Braided) is made into perfection without Flour, perfect for Low Carb option.

Prep Time 10 minutes
Cook Time 45 minutes
Total Time 55 minutes
20 Serving

Ingredients

- 4 Eggs
- 50g (1/3 Cup)Sukrin Plus
- 345g (1,5 Cup) Cream Cheese
- 60g (1/4 Cup)Butter
- 60g (1/4 Cup)Heavy Cream
- 50g (1/4 Cup)Oil
- 1 Cup (100g) Unflavored Protein
- 2/3 Cup (85g) Vanilla Protein
- 1/2 tsp salt
- 1/3 tsp (3g) Baking Soda
- 2 1/2 tsp (12g) Baking Powder
- 1 tsp (4g) Xanthan
- 1/2 of Lemon Zest
- 1/4 Cup (30g) Dried Berries (I have used cranberries)

Instructions

- Heat up the oven to 160C or 320F
- In a separate bowl, mix eggs into fluffiness, then add sugar substitute and mix again.
- Add Cream Cheese and all of the liquid ingredients and mix again
- Once that is properly mixed, add all of the dried ingredients and finish it with mixing it all together.
- Take it our of the mixer and add fresh lemon zest followed by dry cranberries
- Gently hand mix it into the dough, which is then poured into a silicone baking pan, depending on your desired shape.
- Bake for 45 Min
- Bon appetite

Nutrition Info

- Calories: 158
- Total Fat: 13g
- Saturated Fat: 6g
- Trans Fat: 0g
- Unsaturated Fat: 6g
- Cholesterol: 66mg
- Sodium: 241mg
- Carbohydrates: 2g
- Protein: 9g

62. Low Carb Focaccia Bread

Low carb focaccia bread can easily be made as a garlic bread too. Ensure before baking you have shaped the focaccia to be flat and cut little slices half way through the dough. This helps it cook evenly throughout.

Prep Time 15 mins
Cook Time 30 mins
Total Time 45 mins
Servings: Loaf

Ingredients

- 50 g coconut flour
- 5 tbsp psyllium husk
- 2 tsp baking powder
- 1 tsp salt
- 4 eggs - medium
- 250 ml boiling water

Instructions

- Place the coconut flour, psyllium husks, baking powder and salt into a large mixing bowl and stir until combined.
- Add the eggs and mix. The mixture will be a very firm 'play-dough' like consistency so don't work it too hard at this point.
- Add the cup of boiling water and mix until thoroughly combined.
- Form into a focaccia shape and place on a baking tray lined with baking paper. Using a sharp knife, make diagonal cuts through

the dough, sprinkle with plenty of salt, rosemary and place olives on top of the dough.
- Bake at 180C for 25-30 minutes. It is cooked when the centre is no longer 'spongy'.
- Serve hot with butter, cold with cheese, avocado slices, tomatoes, labna, etc.

Notes

- To ensure you avoid any 'eggy' taste, add plenty of flavours such as rosemary, garlic, salt etc.* Psyllium husk 100% fibre and once added to water, swell and thicken.
- Always drink plenty of fluids when taking psyllium, as the husks will swell and absorb liquids from your gut as it transits through.

Nutrition Info

- Calories 528 Calories from Fat 234
- Total Fat 26g 40%
- Total Carbohydrates 58g 19%
- Dietary Fiber 42g 168%
- Sugars 5.9g
- Protein 31g 62%

63. Soul Bread Sesame Rolls

Have you tried Soul Bread yet? It just might be the most innovative and delicious low carb bread recipe around. These little keto rolls are perfect for making burgers, sliders and other sandwiches.

Prep Time 15 mins
Cook Time 35 mins
Total Time 50 mins
Servings: 12 small rolls

Ingredients

- 8 ounces cream cheese softened
- 3 tbsp butter melted
- 2 1/2 tbsp avocado oil
- 2 1/2 tbsp whipping cream
- 2 eggs
- 1 egg white
- 1 cup plus 3 tbsp unflavoured whey protein powder
- 1 1/2 tsp baking powder
- 1/2 tsp xanthan gum
- 1/2 tsp garlic powder
- 1/4 plus 1/8 tsp salt
- 1/4 tsp baking soda
- 1/4 tsp cream of tartar
- Toasted sesame seeds

Instructions

- Preheat oven to 325F and grease a muffin top pan or a square brownie pan very well. You can also use a muffin pan.

- In a large bowl, beat together cream cheese, butter, avocado oil, whipping cream, eggs, and egg white.
- In another bowl, whisk together the protein powder, baking powder, xanthan gum, garlic powder, salt, baking soda, and cream of tartar. Break up any clumps with a fork.
- Add dry ingredients to the cream cheese mixture and fold in by hand until just combined. Do not over mix.
- Fill the cavities of prepared pan to almost full (for the muffin top pan, you may need to work in batches). Sprinkle tops with toasted sesame seeds.
- Bake 25 to 35 minutes, until golden brown on top and firm to the touch. Remove and let cool in pan 15 minutes, then flip out onto a wire rack to cool completely. *If using a muffin top pan, they won't take as long to bake. Keep your eye on them!

Nutrition Info

Calories 175 Calories from Fat 130
Total Fat 14.42g 22%
Cholesterol 67mg 22%
Total Carbohydrates 2.5g 1%
Dietary Fiber 0.33g 1%
Protein 9.34g 19%

64. Keto Pull Apart Clover Rolls

Keto Pull Apart Clover Rolls are the best low carb gluten free rolls that I have ever made! Soft, buttery, cheesy rolls that pull apart into three sections like a three leaf clover

Prep Time 7 mins
Cook Time 20 mins
Total Time 27 mins
Servings: 4

Ingredients

- 1 ½ cup blanched almond flour or can also use 1/3 cup coconut flour instead
- 1 ½ tsp baking powder
- 1 ½ cup shredded Mozzarella cheese
- 2 ounces cream cheese
- ¼ cup grated Parmesan cheese
- 2 lg eggs

Instructions

- Grease or spray with non-stick oil spray a muffin pan and preheat oven to 350 F.
- In a mixing bowl combine the almond flour and the baking powder, mix well. Set aside.
- Melt the shredded Mozzarella and the cream cheese on the stove top (or in the microwave for 1 minute) until melted.

- Once the cheese has melted, add flour mix, and eggs. Mix together.
- Grease hands and knead dough to form a sticky ball. Place the dough ball on a large sheet of baking paper or a silicon mat.
- Slice the dough ball into fourths. Then slice each quarter into 6 small pieces.
- Roll the small pieces into balls, and lightly roll the balls in a bowl of the Parmesan cheese to lightly coat them with Parmesan (this helps them be able to pull apart easily).
- Add 3 of the dough balls to each muffin cup in the muffin pan (this makes the 3 leaf clover).
- Bake at 350 F for 20 minutes or until golden brown. Remove from oven and allow to cool slightly before serving.

Nutrition Info

- Calories 283 Calories from Fat 189
- Total Fat 21g 32%
- Saturated Fat 8g 40%
- Total Carbohydrates 6g 2%
- Dietary Fiber 2g 8%
- Sugars 1g
- Protein 16g 32%

65. Low Carb Bagels-Gluten Free Onion Sesame

Prep/Cook Time:

Ingredients

- 2 1/2 cups mozzerella cheese
- 2 ounces cream cheese
- 3 eggs
- 1 1/2 cups almond flour
- 1 Tablespoon onion powder
- 1/2 teaspoon salt
- 1 Tablespoon sesame seeds

Instructions

- Preheat oven to 400 degrees F.
- Over a double boiler, melt mozzarella cheese and cream cheese together.
- When melted, stir together and beat in 2 eggs.
- In a separate bowl, add almond flour, onion powder, and salt. Stir to combine.
- Pour flour mixture into cheese/egg mixture and mix well.
- Using wet hands, take a small handful (about the size of an orange) and form into a ball. Flatten and make a hole in the center.
- Lay bagels on parchment lined baking sheet.
- Beat the remaining egg and brush over the bagels.
- Sprinkle sesame seeds over bagels and place in oven. Bake for 12 minutes, until golden brown. Remove and allow to cool on the baking sheet.

Nutrition Info
- Calories: 287
- Total Fat: 23g
- Saturated Fat: 7g
- Trans Fat: 0g
- Unsaturated Fat: 14g
- Cholesterol: 105mg
- Sodium: 401mg
- Carbohydrates: 7g
- Fiber: 3g
- Sugar: 2g
- Protein: 15g

66. Keto + Low Carb Cornbread Muffins

These muffins are completely corn-free, but they are reminiscent of real cornbread muffins without the high carb count. They're perfect as a side, breakfast, or snack!

Prep Time: 15 minutes
Cook Time: 25 minutes
Total Time: 40 minutes
Servings: 12

Ingredients

- 3 eggs, slightly beaten
- 1/2 cup heavy whipping cream
- 1/2 cup unsweetened coconut milk (from a carton, not a jar)
- 5 tbsp salted butter, melted
- 3 oz cream cheese, softened
- 1 cup (128g) coconut flour
- 1/4 cup (30g) almond meal
- 3 tbsp (27g) Swerve Confectioners
- 1 1/2 tsp baking powder
- 1/8 tsp salt

Instructions

- Pre-heat oven to 350 F.
- If you're using a silicone muffin pan like I did, you don't need to grease the pan. However, if you're not using silicone, I recommend lightly greasing it or using liners for easy removal.
- In a large bowl, combine eggs, heavy whipping cream, coconut milk, melted butter (cooled slightly), and cream cheese. Using a hand mixer, mix everything until the cream cheese is well-incorporated. (It's okay if you have a few small flecks remaining.) Set aside.
- In a medium-sized bowl, combine coconut flour, almond meal, Swerve Confectioners, baking powder, and salt. Mix thoroughly.
- Add dry ingredients to wet and mix thoroughly using your hand mixer.
- Evenly distribute the batter across the holes, pressing the batter down a bit with the back of a spoon. (The batter is thick and easily forms pockets.) They will be about 80% full.
- Place in the oven and bake for 20-25 minutes until the edges start to brown and an inserted toothpick comes out mostly clean. Do not overbake. The center should still be slightly soft (but not uncooked) when you pull the pan out of the oven.
- Cool and enjoy!

Nutrition Info

Calories 169 Calories from Fat 126; Total Fat 14g 22%; Saturated Fat 8g 40%; Cholesterol 64mg 21%; Sodium 105mg 4%; Potassium 105mg 3%; Total Carbohydrates 7.8g 3%; Dietary Fiber 3.7g 15%; Sugars 0g; Protein 4g 8%

67. Easy Low Carb Cheese Bombs

Make the perfect keto or low carb snack or appetizer with this recipe for Easy Low Carb Cheese Bombs that are so good to eat!

Prep Time 10 mins
Cook Time 12 mins
Total Time 22 mins
Servings: 4

Ingredients

- 12 Low Carb Biscuits
- 1 Egg
- 2 tbsp Milk
- 8 ounces Cheddar Cheese

Instructions

- Start by preheating your oven to 400 degrees. Also, prep one or two baking sheets for nonstick.
- In a small bowl, whip together your egg and milk. Set this bowl aside while you work.
- Prepare your biscuits as indicated in the recipe that you choose to use. Do not bake the biscuits. If you have not done as of yet, cut out each biscuit from the dough using a round cookie cutter. Place a cheese cube in the center of each cut out pieces of dough. The form the dough around the cheese to make a ball or bomb.
- Place the ball or bomb on to the prepared baking sheet. Then brush the egg and milk mixture on the surface of the ball.
- Lastly, bake for 10-12 minutes until they being to brown.
- You can brush with garlic butter if you desire. Allow to cool a bit before serving.

68. Sunflower Pumpkin Seed Psyllium Bread

A low carb gluten free pumpkin sunflower seed psyllium bread. It's packed with hearty seeds and fiber. Enjoy it as a snack or along with a meal.

Prep Time 5 minutes
Cook Time 1 hour 10 minutes
Total Time 1 hour 15 minutes
Servings 10 people

Ingredients

- 1/2 cup whole psyllium husks finely ground, 60g
- 1/4 cup chia seeds 40g
- 1/4 cup pumpkin seeds 40g
- 1/4 cup sunflower seeds 40g
- 2 tablespoons flaxseed meal (15g) or sesame seed flour
- 1 teaspoon baking powder
- 1/4 teaspoon salt
- 3 tablespoons coconut oil melted
- 1 1/4 cup egg whites (300g) I used pasteurized in a carton
- 1/2 cup almond milk

Instructions

- In large mixing bowl, stir together psyllium, chia, pumpkin seeds, sunflower seeds, flax, baking powder, and salt.
- Stir in coconut oil.
- Blend in egg whites and almond milk being careful not to over mix.

- When thickened, spread out into a greased or lined 8x4-inch loaf pan.
- Bake for about 70 minutes at 325°F or until internal temperature reaches about 215°F.

Nutrition Info

- Calories 155 Calories from Fat 72
- Total Fat 8g 12%
- Saturated Fat 4g 20%
- Cholesterol 0mg 0%
- Sodium 126mg 5%
- Potassium 153mg 4%
- Total Carbohydrates 14g 5%
- Dietary Fiber 11g 44%
- Sugars 0g
- Protein 5g 10%

69. 1-2-3 Bread (Dairy-Free)

Prep/Cook Time: 50 minutes

Ingreients

- 1 teaspoon aluminium-free baking powder
- 2 cups = 480 ml = 8 oz = 230 g almond flour
- 3 extra large organic eggs

Intructions

- Preheat the oven to 300 °F (150 °C).
- Mix the baking powder with the almond flour in a medium bowl.
- In a large bowl, beat the eggs with an electric mixer until almost white and fluffy. The mixture will expand remarkably.
- Fold the almond flour mixture gently to the eggs preferably with a rubber spatula until there are no lumps.
- Put the dough into a generously greased small loaf pan or a silicone loaf pan and level the top with a rubber spatula.
- Bake for 30–40 minutes or until a stick inserted into the loaf comes out dry.
- Let cool and cut into slices.

Nutrition Info

1585 kcal
Protein 73.0 g
Fat 133.0 g

70. Simple and Fluffy Gluten-Free Low-Carb Bread

Prep/Cook Time: 50 minutes

Ingredients

- 1/2 cup = 120 ml = 45 g unflavored whey protein powder
- 2 teaspoons aluminium-free baking powder
- 1/2 cup = 120 ml = 125 g almond butter (natural, unsweetened)
- 4 extra large organic eggs

Intructions

- Preheat the oven to 300 °F (150 °C).
- Mix well the whey protein and baking powder in a small bowl.
- Beat the almond butter with an electric mixer in a large bowl until creamy.
- Add one egg at a time beating well after each addition until the batter is smooth, fluffy and bubbly.
- Combine the whey protein mixture with the almond butter mixture and beat well until creamy.
- Pour the batter in a 9 X 5 inch (23 X 13 cm) silicone loaf pan.
- Bake for 30–40 minutes.
- Let cool, remove from the pan and cut into slices.

71. Keto Paleo Low-Carb Stuffing

A paleo-friendly, low-carb, keto stuffing made with homemade coconut flour bread. Savory and delicious for everyone at the holiday dinner table.

Prep time: 20 mins
Cook time: 30 mins
Total time: 50 mins
Serves: 12

Ingredients

- 1 loaf low-carb coconut flour bread
- ¼ cup fresh parsley
- 2 tablespoons tallow, coconut oil or red palm oil
- ½ red onion (200 grams), diced
- 4 celery sticks (200 grams), diced
- 2 teaspoons dried thyme leaves
- 1 teaspoon dried rosemary
- ½ teaspoon dried ground sage
- ¼ teaspoon black pepper
- ¼ teaspoon Himalayan rock salt
- ¼ teaspoon ground ginger
- ¼ teaspoon ground cinnamon
- ¾ cup homemade beef broth
- ¼ cup stevia-sweetened ginger ale (soda), or additional beef broth

Instructions

- Roughly chop fresh-baked bread into 1 inch chunks (it doesn't have to be perfect). Place the pieces on a large baking sheet and place in the oven (do not turn it on!). Keep it there for 24-48 hours. If it's still moist, let it sit in a 170F oven for about 1 hour or so. The bread should be a bit more moist than croutons, but not soft. This step will help the bread retain its shape in the stuffing, so don't skip it! Alternatively, you can dehydrate in your dehydrator, 130F for 24 hours.
- Place the bread chunks in a large bowl, toss with fresh parsley and set aside.
- Preheat oven to 350F and lightly grease a 2.3 L/2.5 qt. casserole dish with a dab of tallow, coconut oil or red palm oil.
- Heat tallow in a large pan on medium-high heat. Add onion and cook until soft, about 5 minutes. Add celery, thyme, rosemary, sage, pepper, salt, ginger and cinnamon. Cook for another 3 minutes.
- Remove from heat and add vegetable mixture to bread and toss to combine being sure not to over mix.
- Now, combine the beef broth and stevia-sweetened soda in a small dish. Pour the mixture over top of the bread. Again, be sure not to over mix, just toss, then add to the prepared casserole dish.
- Cover and bake in preheated oven for 30 minutes.
- Remove from the oven and let sit with the cover on for 5 minutes.

Nutrition Info

Calories: 234; Calories from Fat: 158.4; Total Fat: 17.6 g; Saturated Fat: 12.2 g; Cholesterol: 55 mg; Sodium: 169 mg; Carbs: 11.1 g; Dietary Fiber: 5.7 g; Net Carbs: 5.4 g; Sugars: 3.1 g; Protein: 7.7 g

72. Low Carb Paleo Tortillas Recipe - 3 Ingredient Coconut Flour Wraps

If you're looking for easy coconut flour recipes, try paleo low carb tortillas with coconut flour. Just 3 ingredients in these keto paleo coconut wraps!

Prep Time 5 minutes
Cook Time 10 minutes
Total Time 15 minutes
Servings 8" tortillas

Ingredients

- 1/2 cup Coconut flour
- 6 large Eggs (up to 7-8, see notes)
- 1 1/4 cup Unsweetened almond milk (up to 1 1/2 cup, see notes; can also use any milk of choice - use coconut milk beverage for nut-free)
- 3/4 tsp Sea salt (optional)
- 1 tbsp Gelatin powder (optional - for more pliable, sturdy tortillas)
- 1/2 tsp Cumin (optional)
- 1/2 tsp Paprika (optional)

Instructions

- In a large bowl, whisk all ingredients together until smooth. Let the batter sit for a minute or two to account for the natural thickening caused by coconut flour. The batter should be very

runny right before cooking - it should pour easily (add more almond milk and eggs in *equal* proportions if needed to achieve this). If you are using the optional gelatin, add an extra 1/4 cup almond milk.
- Heat a small skillet (about 8 in (20 cm) diameter) over medium to medium-high heat and grease lightly (use oil of choice or an oil mister). Pour 1/4 cup (60 mL) of batter onto the skillet and immediately, rapidly tilt in different directions to evenly distribute, like making crepes.
- Cook, covered with a lid, until the edges are golden and you see bubbles forming in the middle. The edges will curl inward when you lift the lid (about 1-2 minutes). Flip over, cover again, and cook until browned on the other side (1-2 more minutes). Repeat until the batter is used up.

Nutrition Info

- Calories 55
- Fat 3g
- Protein 5g
- Total Carbs 4g
- Net Carbs 1g
- Fiber 3g
- Sugar 1g

73. Paleo Gluten-Free Low Carb English Muffin Recipe in a Minute

A paleo low carb English muffin recipe that's soft and buttery inside, crusty on the outside. These gluten-free English muffins are easy to make in 2 minutes, with 5 ingredients!

Prep Time 2 minutes
Cook Time 3 minutes
Total Time 5 minutes

Ingredients

- 3 tbsp Blanched almond flour
- 1/2 tbsp Coconut flour
- 1 tbsp Butter (or ghee, or coconut oil)
- 1 large Egg (or equivalent egg whites)
- 1 pinch Sea salt
- 1/2 tsp Gluten-free baking powder

Instructions

- Melt ghee (or butter) in a microwave or oven safe ramekin or other container, about 4 in (10 cm) diameter with a flat bottom. This takes about 30 seconds. (If using the oven only, you can melt it in the oven while it preheats. Remove once melted.)
- Add the remaining ingredients and stir until well combined. Let sit for a minute to allow the mixture to thicken.
- Microwave method: Microwave for about 90 seconds, until firm.
- Oven method: Bake for about 15 minutes at 350 degrees F (177 degrees C), until the top is firm and spring-y to the touch.

- Run a knife along the edge and flip over a plate to release. Slice in half, then toast in the toaster.

Recipe Notes

For more container options, see the list right above the recipe card (scroll up).

If you prefer more/smaller slices, you can also make it in a mug instead of a ramekin, then just pop those in the toaster in batches.

Serving size: 2 large slices (entire recipe)

Nutrition Info
- Calories 307
- Fat 27g
- Protein 12g
- Total Carbs 8g
- Net Carbs 4g
- Fiber 4g
- Sugar 2g

74. Low Carb Chelsea Buns

Low-carb Chelsea buns are so light and fluffy, who knew they could be this easy to make (and enjoy).

Prep Time15 mins
Cook Time20 mins
Total Time35 mins
Servings:4

Ingredients

- 200 g almond meal/flour
- 40 g psyllium husk
- 2 tsp baking powder
- 5 tbsp granulated sweetener of choice or more, to your taste
- 4 egg whites
- 1 tsp vanilla
- 250 ml boiling water

Cinnamon filling

- 2 tsp ground cinnamon
- 2 tsp granulated sweetener of choice
- lemon zest optional

Glaze

- 4 tbsp powdered sweetener
- 1 tsp vanilla optional
- water enough to make a liquid glaze

Instructions

Low Carb Chelsea Bun Dough

- Place all the dry ingredients together in a bowl and mix well.
- Make a hole in the middle of the dry ingredients and add the egg whites and vanilla. Mix just a little so you can't see the egg whites any more.
- Add 1/3 the boiling water gently and slowly, mix. Add another 1/3, mix. Add the final 1/3 and mix until it looks like a sticky dough.
- If the dough looks too wet, add an extra tablespoon of psyllium husk, if too dry, add a teaspoon of water at a time.
- Pour the dough onto a large sheet of baking parchment/paper. Place another piece of baking parchment/paper on top.
- Press out with your hands until it is a rectangle shape and 1cm / 1/2 inch thick.

Cinnamon filling

- Mix the cinnamon and sweetener together and sprinkle all over the rolled dough.
- Using the baking parchment/paper, start to roll the dough up along the longest side.
- Continue to roll it into one long roll, then cut into even slices.
- Place each slice in a ring tin that has been oiled and lined.
- Bake at 180C/350F for 20-30 minutes, or until golden, and baked in the centre of each Chelsea bun.

Glaze

- Mix the powdered sweetener, vanilla and water together to make a liquid glaze.

- Drizzle, pour or spoon all over.
- Enjoy warm or cold.

Nutrition Info

- Calories 246 Calories from Fat 167
- Total Fat 18.6g 29%
- Total Carbohydrates 13.7g 5%
- Dietary Fiber 8.2g 33%
- Sugars 1.6g
- Protein 10g

75. Cinnamon Raisin Swirl Bread

A low carb Cinnamon Raisin Swirl Bread that does the original justice! Enjoy this naturally sweet and healthy treat for your holiday brunch or breakfast.

Prep Time 20 mins
Cook Time 1 hr 10 mins
Total Time 1 hr 30 mins
Servings: 1 loaf

Ingredients

Filling:

- 1 tbsp Swerve Sweetener
- 1 tsp ground cinnamon

Bread:

- 1/2 cup coconut flour
- 1/2 cup almond flour
- 6 tbsp psyllium husk powder
- 1/4 cup California raisins chopped fine
- 2 tbsp Swerve Sweetener
- 1 tbsp baking powder
- 1/2 tsp ground cinnamon
- 1/4 tsp salt
- 2 cups egg whites (liquid egg whites work well but you can also measure out whites from regular eggs. It will be 8 to 12 whites, depending on the size)
- 4 tbsp melted butter divided
- 2 tbsp apple cider vinegar
- 3/4 cup hot water (almost boiling)

Instructions

- Preheat oven to 350F and grease a 9x5 inch loaf pan. Grease 2 large pieces of parchment paper.
- In a small bowl, whisk together the sweetener and cinnamon. Set aside.
- In a large bowl, whisk together the coconut flour, almond flour, psyllium husk powder, chopped raisins, sweetener, baking powder, cinnamon and salt.
- Add egg whites, 3 tbsp of the melted butter and the apple cider vinegar. Stir to combine. Slowly stir in hot water until dough expands.
- Turn dough out onto one of the pieces of greased parchment and pat into a rough rectangle. Top with other piece of parchment

and roll out to about 8x 12 inches. Brush with about half of the remaining melted butter and sprinkle with cinnamon filling. Roll up tightly and place seam-side-down in prepared loaf pan.
- Brush with remaining butter. Bake 60 to 70 minutes, until golden brown and firm to the touch. Remove from oven and tent with foil. Let cool in pan (this will help keep it from deflating). Once cool, transfer it to a cutting board or serving plate.

Nutrition Info
- Calories 132 Calories from Fat 59
- Total Fat 6.58g 10%
- Saturated Fat 3.27g 16%
- Cholesterol 10mg 3%
- Sodium 283mg 12%
- Total Carbohydrates 12.36g 4%
- Dietary Fiber 6.02g 24%
- Protein 6.28g 13%

76. Keto Cheddar Bay Biscuits

These keto cheddar bay biscuits taste so much like Red Lobster biscuits! Try this copycat recipe for savory, cheesy, and EASY keto dinner rolls.

Prep time: 5 mins
Cook time: 25 mins
Total time: 30 mins

Ingredients:

- 2 cups almond flour (what we used)
- 2 teaspoons baking powder
- 1/2 teaspoon Himalayan salt
- 1/2 teaspoon garlic powder
- 1/4 teaspoon ground black pepper
- 4 tablespoons grass-fed unsalted butter, chilled and cut into small pieces
- 4 tablespoons heavy whipping cream
- 2 large eggs, beaten
- 4 ounces white cheddar cheese, shredded
- 2 ounces sharp yellow cheddar cheese, shredded
- 1 tablespoon dried parsley

Instructions

- Preheat oven to 350 degrees. Line a baking sheet with parchment or a silicone baking liner.

- In a large mixing bowl, blend all dry ingredients. Add butter and crumble with a fork (or your hands, if they're cold) until incorporated well into the dry mix.
- Add heavy cream in small amounts, mixing well between each addition. Stir eggs into the mixture. Mix white cheddar into the batter until it forms a doughy consistency, then gently add in yellow cheddar.
- Scoop 8 even portions of dough onto your prepared baking sheet. (You can also roll into balls instead if you want rounder biscuits.)
- Bake for 20 minutes, or until browned on the bottom.
- Serve warm, or cool completely and store in a covered container. Reheat gently in a toaster oven when ready to serve again.

Nutrition Info

calories 350
fat (grams) 32
sat. fat (grams) 12
carbs (grams) 6.2

77. Parmesan & Tomato Keto Bread Buns

Prep Time: 10-15 minutes
Total Time: 55-60 minutes
Servings: 5

Ingredients

Dry ingredients:

- 3/4 cup almond flour (75 g/ 2.7 oz)
- 2 1/2 tbsp psyllium husk powder (20 g/ 0.7 oz)
- 1/4 cup coconut flour (30 g/ 1.1 oz)
- 1/4 cup packed cup flax meal (38 g/ 1.3 oz)
- 1 tsp cream of tartar or apple cider vinegar
- 1/2 tsp baking soda
- 2/3 cup grated Parmesan cheese (60 g/ 2.1 oz)
- 1/3 cup chopped sun-dried tomatoes (37 g/ 1.3 oz)
- 1/4 - 1/2 tsp pink sea salt
- 2 tbsp sesame seeds (18 g/ 0.6 oz) - or use 2 tbsp sunflower, flax, poppy seeds, or 1 tbsp caraway seeds

Wet ingredients:

- 3 large egg whites
- 1 large egg
- 1 cups boiling water (240 ml/ 8 fl oz)

Instructions

- Preheat the oven to 175 °C/ 350 °F (fan assisted). Use a kitchen scale to measure all the ingredients and add them to a mixing bowl (apart from the sesame seeds which are used for topping): almond flour, coconut flour, flax meal, psyllium husk powder, cream of tartar, baking soda, salt, parmesan cheese and sun dried tomatoes. Mix all the dry ingredients together. Parmesan & Tomato Keto Bread Buns

- Add the egg whites and eggs and process well using a mixer until the dough is thick.
- The reason you shouldn't use only whole eggs is that the buns wouldn't rise with so many egg yolks in. Don't waste them - use them for making Home-made Mayo, Easy Hollandaise Sauce or Lemon Curd. Parmesan & Tomato Keto Bread Buns
- Add boiling water and process until well combined. Parmesan & Tomato Keto Bread Buns
- Using a spoon, divide the keto buns mix into 5 and roll into buns using your hands. Place them on a non-stick baking tray or on parchment paper. They will grow in size, so make sure to leave some space between them. You can even use small tart trays.
- Top each of the buns with sesame seeds (or any other seeds) and gently press them into the dough, so they don't fall out. Place in the oven and cook for about 45 - 50 minutes until golden on top. Parmesan & Tomato Keto Bread Buns
- Remove from the oven, let the tray cool down and place the buns on a rack to cool to room temperature. Parmesan & Tomato Keto Bread Buns
- Enjoy just like you would regular bread — with butter, ham or cheese! Parmesan & Tomato Keto Bread Buns Store in a tupperware for 2-3 days or freeze for up to 3 months.

Note: You Can make 5 regular/large buns as per recipe, or up to 10 small buns.

Nutrition Info

Calories 261 kcal
Net carbs 4.9 grams
Protein 14.5 grams
Fat 18.9 grams

78. Keto Croissants

Fluffy with a crispy crust, these keto-style croissants will hit the spot when you are looking for something doughy on the side!

8 Servings
Prep Time 10 mins
Cook Time 13 mins
Total Time 23 mins

Ingredients

- 3 cups mozzarella cheese, shredded
- 2 oz cream cheese
- 3 egg whites
- ½ cup coconut flour
- 2 tbsp butter, melted
- 1 tbsp psyllium husk
- 2 tbsp sparkling water (room temperature)
- salt to taste

Instructions

- Preheat oven to 385°F and line baking sheet with parchment paper.
- Beat the egg whites until soft peaks form.
- Add cheese and cream cheese to a large microwavable bowl, stir and microwave until melted.
- Stir in the beaten egg whites, coconut flour, psyllium husk, and pinch of salt.
- Knead with hands until a dough-like consistency is reached, add sparkling water, and continue kneading.
- Note: If the dough becomes hard, microwave it for 10-15 seconds.
- Place dough between two sheets of parchment paper and spread with rolling pin to about ½ inches thickness.
- Brush half of the melted butter onto the dough.
- With a pizza cutter, start dividing the dough into 4 equal squares and further cut each square into two triangles that have a bottom approximately 4 inches wide.
- Roll the triangles upward, starting at the widest part, and gradually curve into a crescent shape.
- Place croissants onto baking sheet at least 2 inches apart.
- Brush remaining butter on top and bake for 12 minutes or until golden brown.

Nutrition Info

Servings 8; Calories 248; Total Fat 17.2g 27%; Net Carbohydrate 7.2g 3%; Dietary Fiber 3.8g 16%; Protein 16g 32%

79. Cinnamon Almond Flour Bread {Paleo}

This delicious cinnamon almond flour bread is a versatile low carb, gluten free and paleo bread recipe the whole family loves! Simple ingredients, nourishing, soft and delicious.

Prep Time: 10
Cook Time: 30 minutes
Total Time: 40 minutes
Serving: 8

Ingredients

- 2 cups fine blanched almond flour? (I use Bob's Red Mill)
- 2 tbsp coconut flour
- 1/2 tsp sea salt
- 1 tsp baking soda
- 1/4 cup Flax seed meal or chia meal ?(ground chia or flaxseed, see notes for how to make your own)
- 5 Eggs and 1 egg white whisked ??together
- 1.5 tsp Apple cider vinegar or lemon juice
- 2 tbsp maple syrup or honey
- 2-3 tbsp of clarified butter (melted) or Coconut oil; divided. Vegan butter also works
- 1 tbsp cinnamon plus extra for topping
- Optional chia seed to sprinkle of top before baking

Instructions

Preheat oven to 350F. Line an 8×4 bread pan with parchment paper at the bottom and grease the sides.

- In a large bowl, mix together your almond flour, coconut flour, salt, baking soda, flaxseed meal or chia meal, and 1/2 tablespoon of cinnamon.
- In another small bowl, whisk together your eggs and egg white. Then add in your maple syrup (or honey), apple cider vinegar, and melted butter (1.5 to 2 tbsp).
- Mix wet ingredients into dry. Be sure to remove any clumps that might have occurred from the almond flour or coconut flour.
- Pour batter into a your greased loaf pan.
- Bake at 350º for 30-35 minutes, until a toothpick inserted into center of loaf comes out clean. Mine too around 35 minutes but I am at altitude.
- Remove from and oven.
- Next, whisk together the other 1 to 2 tbsp of melted butter (or oil) and mix it with 1/2 tbsp of cinnamon. Brush this on top of your cinnamon almond flour bread.
- Cool and serve or store for later.

Notes

- For storage, it's best to keep wrapped in foil or ziplock in fridge. The bread freezes well for meal prep.
- If you you use a larger pan, the loaf slices will be less fluffy but equally delicious.
- To make the flaxseed or chia meal, simply place the the flaxseeds or chia seeds in a coffee grinder and grind until a fine meal is formed.

Nutrition Info

Serving Size: 1; Calories Per Serving: 221; 24% Total Fat 15.4g' 13% Dietary Fiber 3.1g; Sugars 3.7g ;19% Protein 9.3g; 0% Vitamin C 0mg

80. Low Carb Gluten Free Cranberry Bread

A delicious gluten free low carb cranberry bread with fresh cranberries. This sugar-free bread uses a combination of stevia and erythritol sweeteners.

Prep Time 10 minutes
Cook Time 1 hour 15 minutes
Total Time 1 hour 25 minutes
Servings 12 people

Ingredients

- 2 cups almond flour
- 1/2 cup powdered erythritol or Swerve, see Note
- 1/2 teaspoon Steviva stevia powder see Note
- 1 1/2 teaspoons baking powder
- 1/2 teaspoon baking soda
- 1 teaspoon salt
- 4 tablespoons unsalted butter melted (or coconut oil)
- 1 teaspoon blackstrap molasses optional (for brown sugar flavor)
- 4 large eggs at room temperature
- 1/2 cup coconut milk
- 1 bag cranberries 12 ounces

Instructions

- Preheat oven to 350 degrees; grease a 9-by-5 inch loaf pan and set aside.
- In a large bowl, whisk together flour, erythritol, stevia, baking powder, baking soda, and salt; set aside.
- In a medium bowl, combine butter, molasses, eggs, and coconut milk.
- Mix dry mixture into wet mixture until well combined.
- Fold in cranberries. Pour batter into prepared pan.
- Bake until a toothpick inserted in the center of the loaf comes clean, about 1 hour and 15 minutes.
- Transfer pan to a wire rack; let bread cool 15 minutes before removing from pan.

Nutrition Info

- Calories 179 Calories from Fat 135
- Total Fat 15g 23%
- Saturated Fat 4g 20%
- Cholesterol 72mg 24%
- Sodium 276mg 12%
- Potassium 38mg 1%
- Total Carbohydrates 7g 2%
- Dietary Fiber 2g 8%
- Sugars 1g
- Protein 6.4g 13%

81. Rosemary Keto Bagels

Prep/Cook Time: 55 minutes (10 minutes active)
Serves: 4

Ingredients:

- 1 1/2 cups almond flour
- 3/4 teaspoon baking soda
- 3/4 teaspoon xanthan gum
- 1/4 teaspoon salt
- 3 tablespoons psyllium husk powder
- 1 whole egg
- 3 egg whites
- 1/2 cup warm water
- 1 tablespoon rosemary, chopped
- Avocado oil

Instructions:

- Preheat oven to 250F.
- Mix almond flour, xanthan gum, baking soda and salt together in a bowl.
- In a separate bowl, whisk eggs and warm water together. Stir in psyllium husk until there are no clumps.
- Add liquid ingredients to dry ingredients.
- Coat bagel mold with avocado oil.
- Press dough into mold.
- Sprinkle rosemary on top.
- Place in oven and bake for 45 minutes.
- Remove and cool for 15 minutes before slicing.

Nutrition Info

- Calories: 285
- Protein: 13g
- Carbs: 12g
- Fiber: 7.5g
- Net Carbs: 4.5g
- Sugar: 1.75g
- Fat: 22.5g
- Saturated Fat: 2g

82. Homemade Nut and Seed Paleo Bread

Prep Time: 10 min
Cook Time: 40 min
Total Time: 50 minutes
Serving: 12 -15 slices

Ingredients

- 1 1/4 cup almond flour
- 5 eggs (6 if you want extra fluffy)
- 1/3 cup coconut oil or avocado oil
- 1 tsp white vinegar or apple cider vinegar
- 1/2 tsp sea salt
- dash of black pepper
- Optional 1 tsp spice mix of choice (garlic, rosemary, Italian, etc.).
- 1 – 2 tsp poppyseed (plus extra for topping)
- 3 to 4 tbsp tapioca flour (if you are using more egg, add 4 tbsp).

- 1/2 tsp baking soda
- 1/4 cup chia meal (just grind chia seed in a coffee grinder or blender) or use ground flaxseed
- Pumpkin seed for topping and Extra poppyseed

Instructions

- Preheat oven to 350. Grease a 9×5 bread pan or line with parchment paper. Set aside. For higher rising bread, use an 8×4 pan.
- In a small bowl, whisk your eggs, oil, and vinegar.
- In another bowl, combine your flours, poppyseed, and seasonings.
- Add your wet ingredients to dry ingredients and mix thoroughly.
- Pour batter into greased pan and top with additional pumpkin seeds and and additional poppyseed.
- Bake covered for 20 minutes. Then uncover and continue to bake for additional 15-20 more or golden and knife in the centre comes out clean.
- Should be around 35-45 minutes all together depending on your oven. If you used 8×4 or are baking at higher elevation, you might need to bake longer.
- Remove from oven and let cool.
- Wrap the paleo bread in foil or plastic wrap, slice and store in container. Keeps well in fridge for up to 7 days or freezer for up to 3 months.

83. Keto Low Carb Mug Bread

A quick an easy bread to make that is keto and low carb friendly

Prep Time 2 mins
Cook Time 2 mins
Total Time 4 mins
Servings: 1mug

Ingredients

- Low carb flour alternative Carbalose- 2 tablespoons . OR 1 tablespoon of coconut flour plus 1 tablespoon of almond flour or other alternative flour is suggested.
- Baking powder- 1/2 teaspoon.
- Egg- 1.
- Oil- such as olive oil- 1 tablespoon.
- Seasonings- as desired.
- Optional- grated cheese- 1 tablespoon.

Instructions

- Using a microwave-safe mug and a fork, mix together your flours and baking powder. You can spray your mug for nonstick before adding the dry ingredients if desired.
- In a small bowl, whisk together the remaining ingredients (egg etc).
- Pour the wisked ingredients from the bowl into the mug and lightly blend together using your fork. Avoid lumps without over mixing. A good idea would be to tap the mug on the bottom to help the batter settle into the empty areas of the mug before

baking. Mix enough so that you can get a 'bread in a cup' rather than an 'egg in a cup'.
- Microwave on high for 30 seconds. Rotate the mug and then microwave for another 45 seconds- 1 minute or until the bread seems baked to the eye.
- Carefully remove the mug from the microwave and turn it upside down on a plate or cutting board. The bread should slip out easily. However, you may need to give a quick tap to help it out.
- Slice the bread to your desired thickness.

84. Garlic, Dill & Cheddar Keto Bread

Prep/Cook Time: 55 minutes

Ingredients

1 ½ cups blanched almond flour (165 g)
- 4 large eggs, separated
- 1 tablespoon egg white protein powder (5 g)
- 5 tablespoons unsalted butter, melted and cooled (70 g)
- ¼ teaspoon kosher salt (1.2 ml)
- 3 teaspoons aluminum-free baking powder (15 ml)
- ¼ teaspoon cream of tartar (1.2 ml)
- 1 teaspoon garlic powder (5 ml)
- 1 teaspoon dried dill (5 ml)
- 1 cup grated cheddar cheese (90g)

Instructions

- Preheat oven to 375º F/190º C.

- Lightly grease an 8.5 x 4.5 loaf pan. For easiest release, cover the bottom of the loaf pan with lightly greased parchment paper.

- In a food processor, combine the almond flour, egg yolks, egg white protein powder, butter, salt and baking powder.

- *If making cinnamon & honey bread, add the cinnamon and honey.

- *If making garlic, dill & cheddar bread, add the garlic powder, dill and cheddar.

- Process just until the ingredients come together into a ball of dough.

- In the bowl of an electric mixer, combine the egg whites and cream of tartar. Using the whisk attachment, whisk until the egg whites are big and fluffy and soft peaks form (when the whisk is lifted out of the egg whites, a soft peak should form, then fall slightly).

- Pour 1/3 of the egg whites into the food processor. Pulse until combined, scraping down the sides as needed. Add another 1/3 of the egg whites, and pulse again until combined into a wet batter.

Primal

- Scrape the dough out of the food processor into the bowl with the remaining egg whites. Use a spatula to gently fold the egg whites into the dough. Gently fold and mix until there are no white streaks, but be gentle; the air in the egg whites helps the dough rise into a loaf with a light texture.

- Scrape the batter into the loaf pan. Bake 30 minutes.

- Let cool for at least 30 minutes before removing from the loaf pan. Try to let the loaf cool completely on a wire rack before slicing.

- Primal keto bread keeps for 1 to 2 days on the counter with simply a light towel over the top of it. For longer storage (3 to 5 days), keep the keto bread wrapped lightly in a towel inside a sealed plastic bag in the refrigerator.

Recipe Notes

- If the baking powder is aluminum-free (it usually says so on the front of the can), your baked goods won't have a strange metallic flavor. Another reason to use aluminum-free: baking powder with aluminum can give baked goods a grayish color if the recipe includes an acidic ingredient.

85. Low Carb Pumpkin Bread

Prep Time: 15 minutes
Cook Time: 45 minutes
Total Time: 1 hour
Serving: 20

Ingredients

- 15 oz. can of pumpkin puree
- 2 cups granulated of sugar substitute
- 3 teaspoons of baking powder
- 2 teaspoon vanilla extract
- 3 tablespoons of pumpkin pie spice
- 3 tablespoons of cinnamon powder
- 1/4 teaspoon sea salt
- 10 large eggs
- 3 cups of almond flour
- 1 cup of golden flax meal
- Optional
- Cream Cheese Frosting
- 8 oz package of softened cream cheese
- 4 tablespoons of heavy whipping cream
- 1 cup of sugar-free confectioners sugar

Instructions

- Preheat oven to 350 degrees.
- Grease two 8x4 inch loaf pans well.
- Using an electric mixer, beat the pumpkin puree, sugar substitute, and vanilla extract until well blended.

- Next add in the eggs one at time making sure to beat until fully combined.
- To the wet batter add the almond flour, flax meal, baking powder, spices and salt.
- Note that batter will be thick. Pour the batter into the two prepared pans and bake at 350 degrees for 45 minutes, or until an inserted toothpick comes out clean.

Notes

- This recipe makes two large low carb pumpkin bread loaves and freezes well.

Nutrition Info

- Calories: 200
- Total Fat: 15.8g
- Saturated Fat: 5.5g
- Cholesterol: 59mg
- Sodium: 60mg
- Carbohydrates: 4.8g
- Fiber: 2.9g
- Sugar: 0.8g
- Protein: 6.4g

86. Buttery Low Carb Flatbread

Prep time 5 mins
Cook time 2 mins
Total time 7 mins
Serves: 4

Ingredients

- 1 cup Almond Flour
- 2 tbsp Coconut Flour
- 2 tsp Xanthan Gum
- ½ tsp Baking Powder
- ½ tsp Falk Salt + more to garnish
- 1 Whole Egg + 1 Egg White
- 1 tbsp Water
- 1 tbsp Oil for frying
- 1 tbsp melted Butter-for slathering

Instructions

- Whisk together the dry ingredients (flours, xanthan gum, baking powder, salt) until well combined.
- Add the egg and egg white and beat gently into the flour to incorporate. The dough will begin to form.
- Add the tablespoon of water and begin to work the dough to allow the flour and xanthan gum to absorb the moisture.
- Cut the dough in 4 equal parts and press each section out with cling wrap. Watch the video for instructions!
- Heat a large skillet over medium heat and add oil.
- Fry each flatbread for about 1 min on each side.

- Brush with butter (while hot) and garnish with salt and chopped parsley.

87. Peanut Butter Berry Breakfast Loaf (Low Carb, Gluten Free)

Serving: 12 Slices

Ingredients

- 1/2 cup peanut butter
- 1/4 cup grass fed butter, melted
- 5 pastured eggs
- 1/2 cup coconut milk or almond milk
- 1 tsp vanilla extract
- 1/2 cup almond flour
- 3 tbsp Swerve sweetener (more for a sweeter bread) (I get it here)
- 2 tsp baking powder
- 1/2 tsp sea salt
- 1/2 cup frozen mixed berries

Instructions

- Preheat oven to 350°. Use a silicone loaf pan (Get one here) or line a loaf pan with parchment paper.
- In a large mixing bowl, combine peanut butter, melted butter and eggs. Mix until well combined.
- Add the coconut milk and vanilla extract and mix to combine.

- In a separate mixing bowl, combine the almond flour, sweetener, baking powder and sea salt. mix together until well combined and all chunks of baking powder are broken up.
- Slowly pour the wet mixture into the dry ingredients, mixing as you pour.
- Mix until all ingredients are well incorporated.
- Using a rubber spatula, gently fold the mixed berries into the mixture.
- Pour the batter evenly into the loaf pan.
- Bake for 45 minutes to an hour, checking on it at the 45 minute mark.
- Remove from oven and allow to cool before slicing.
- Pop a couple slices in the toaster and then slather them with delicious grass fed butter!

Nutrition Info
- Calories: 153
- Fat: 13g
- Protein: 5.8g
- Total Carbs: 4.83g
- Fiber: 1.5g
- Net Carbs: 3.33g

88. Hot Ham and Cheese Roll-Ups with Dijon Butter Glaze

Prep/Cook Time: 40 minutes

Ingredients

For the Hot Ham and Cheese Roll-Ups

- 1/4 cup almond flour (get it here)
- 3 tablespoons coconut flour (get it here)
- 1 teaspoon onion powder
- 1 teaspoon garlic powder
- 1 1/2 cup low-moisture, part skim mozzarella cheese, shredded
- 4 tablespoons salted butter
- 2 tablespoons cream cheese
- 1 large pastured egg
- 10 ounces sliced ham
- 1 1/2 cups sharp white cheddar cheese, shredded

For the Dijon Butter Glaze

- 2 tablespoons salted butter
- 1 tablespoon Dijon mustard
- 1 teaspoon Worcestershire sauce
- 1 teaspoon garlic powder
- 1/2 teaspoon dried Italian seasoning

Instructions

- Preheat oven to 375°F.
- In a small mixing bowl, combine almond flour, coconut flour, onion powder and garlic powder.

- In a separate mixing bowl, combine mozzarella cheese, butter, and cream cheese. Microwave for 1 minute and 30 seconds to soften. Mix together until everything is well combined. If if gets stringy or is not quite melted enough, put it back in for another 30 seconds.
- To the cheese mixture, add the dry ingredients and the egg. Mix until all ingredients are well incorporated. If you are having a hard time mixing it, put it back in the microwave for another 20-30 seconds.
- Once the ingredients are combined, spread the dough out on parchment paper or a silpat in a thin and even layer – about 9 1/2 by 13 1/2. If it starts to get sticky, wet your hands a little bit to prevent it from sticking to you.
- Once you have the dough in a nice, even rectangle, sprinkle the cheddar over top, covering all of the dough.
- Next, layer on the ham.
- Roll the dough up tightly lengthwise. This will produce smaller rolls, but you will get almost twice as many. Turn so that the seam is facing down
- Cut the ends off each side of the roll-up to even it out. Then cut it into 1 1/2 slices.
- Place your individual roll-ups in a baking dish.
- Bake for 20-25 minutes or until they are fluffy and golden brown.
- While they are baking, melt the butter and mix it with the Dijon, Worcestershire, garlic powder and Italian seasoning. Fork whisk until all ingredients are well incorporated.
- Take your rolls out of the oven, brush the glaze over top of them. Return them to the oven and bake for an additional 5 minutes.

Nutrition Info

- Calories – 482
- Fat – 41g
- Protein – 25g
- Carbs – 6.8g
- Fiber – 2.8g
- Net Carbs – 4g

89. Low Carb Hot Cross Buns

Low-carb hot cross buns are perfect any time of the year. To ensure they bake evenly, ensure they are not too big and not too thick.

Prep Time15 mins
Cook Time20 mins
Total Time35 mins
Servings:4

Ingredients

Low Carb Hot Cross Buns

- 60 g coconut flour
- 30 g psyllium husks
- 1 tsp baking powder
- 2 tbsp granulated sweetener of choice or more, to your taste
- 1/2 tsp salt
- 1/2 tsp mixed spice
- 1/2 tsp cinnamon

- 1/2 tsp ground cloves
- 4 eggs - medium
- 250 ml boiling water
- raisins/chocolate chips/ cacao nibs optional

Icing

- powdered sweetener icing mix

Instructions

Low Carb Hot Cross Buns

- Mix all the dry ingredients in a mixing bowl.
- Add the eggs and mix.
- Add the boiling water and mix until evenly combined.
- Roll into 8 equal balls and place on a baking tray.
- Bake in a fan assisted oven at 180C/350F for 20-30 minutes until golden on the outside and cooked in the centre.

Icing

- Mark each hot cross bun with a cross using the powdered sweetener confectioners/icing mix and water paste.

Nutrition Info

- Calories 84 Calories from Fat 28
- Total Fat 3.1g 5%
- Total Carbohydrates 8.9g 3%
- Dietary Fiber 6.8g 27%
- Sugars 0.7g

- Protein 5.6g 11%

90. Monkey Bread

Prep/Cook Time: 1 hour, 30 mins

Ingredients

DOUGH:

- 3 cup blanched almond flour (10 oz) (or 1 cup coconut flour or 5 oz)
- 10 TBS psyllium husk powder (no substitutes) (90 grams)
- 4 tsp baking powder
- 2 tsp Celtic sea salt
- 1 cup Swerve (or erythritol and 1 tsp stevia glycerite)
- 8 egg whites (16 whites if using coconut flour)
- 5 TBS apple cider vinegar (2 oz)
- 2 cup BOILING water (14 oz)

FILLING:

- 8 oz cream cheese

TOPPING:

- 8 TBS butter (or coconut oil)
- 1 TBS cinnamon
- 1/2 cup Swerve (or erythritol)

Instructions

- Preheat the oven to 375 degrees F. In a large bowl, combine the flour, psyllium powder (no substitutes: flaxseed meal won't work), baking powder, salt and sweetener. Mix until combined. Add in the eggs and vinegar and combine until a thick dough. Add boiling water into the bowl. Mix until well combined. When you add the water the dough will be very sticky but after mixing for a couple minutes it will firm up.

- Separate dough into 20 equal sized disks. You can spray some more spray on top of the dough to help keep it from sticking to your fingers. Cut cream cheese into 20 squares. Place on square on top of each dough disk and form the disk around the sides of the cream cheese.

- Place 10 of the squares in the bottom of a greased bundt pan with the cream cheese facing up. Sprinkle cinnamon and Swerve on top. Then put the remaining 10 squares inverted on top of the first 10 (making the cream cheese touch). Bake for 55 minutes.

Meanwhile, make the topping.

- Place all ingredients into a medium sized bowl and combine until smooth. After it has baked for 55 minutes, remove and quickly spread topping over the monkey bread. Return to oven and bake for 15 minute. Allow to cool for 20-30 minutes before turning over and removing from bundt pan. Makes 14 servings.

Nutrition Info

- 308 calories
- 21.1g fat
- 2.9g protein
- 28.9 carbs
- trace fiber (28.9g effective carbs)

91. Low Sugar Gluten Free Pumpkin Bread

A moist low sugar, low carb, and gluten free coconut flour pumpkin bread with no added sugars, and a delicious blend of spices to bring out the pumpkin flavor.

Prep time: 10 mins
Cook time: 60 mins
Total time: 1 hour 10 mins

Ingredients

- 1 cup coconut flour
- ½ cup Swerve Sweetener, granulated
- 8 eggs (I used large)
- 1 tsp baking soda
- ½ tsp baking powder
- ½ tsp salt
- 1 tsp Sweetleaf Stevia
- 2 tsp cinnamon
- ½ tsp ginger
- 1 tsp ground cloves

- 2 tbsp vanilla extract
- 1 stick butter
- 1, 15-oz can of pureed Pumpkin

Instructions

- Preheat oven to 350 degrees F, and grease a 9x5 bread pan with butter. (Using oil or butter vs spray helps the bread not to stick to the pan.)
- In a large bowl, mix together the dry ingredients of coconut flour, Swerve Sweetener, baking soda, baking powder, salt, Sweetleaf Stevia, cinnamon, ginger and ground cloves.
- In another bowl, mix together the wet ingredients. When well mixed, add the wet ingredients into the large ingredients and whisk well. (If using a blender, a low-medium blend is fine.)
- Fill the 9x5 bread pan with the pumpkin bread, and bake in the oven until a tooth pick comes out clear. For me, the 50-1 hr mark was perfect.

92. Lemon Poppy Seed Loaf Cake

This Lemon Poppy Seed Loaf Cake is perfect for breakfast or dessert with some fresh berries or a smear of butter. It is low carb, keto, trim healthy mama friendly, gluten grain and sugar-free. It whips up in minutes and stores well for a week! All in all, it is a great healthy choice for your lemon poppy seed craving!

Prep Time 10 mins
Cook Time 1 hr
Total Time 1 hr 10 mins

Servings: 12

Ingredients

- 2/3 cup cottage cheese
- 4 tbsp butter softened
- 1/2 cup Trim Healthy Mama Gentle Sweet or my sweetener
- 4 eggs
- 3 tbsp lemon juice
- 1 1/2 cup almond flour
- 1/2 cup coconut flour
- 2 tsp baking powder
- 1 tsp lemon zest
- 2 tbsp poppy seeds

Instructions

- Preheat oven to 350. Grease a standard loaf pan well with cooking spray.

- Combine the cottage cheese, butter, and sweetener in the food processor. Pulse until smooth. Add the eggs, lemon juice, flours, baking powder, and zest. Pulse until well combined. Add the poppy seeds and pulse until they are evenly distributed in the batter. Transfer the batter to the prepared loaf pan.

- Bake for 55-65 min or until the center feels firm when lightly pressed and the edges are deep golden brown.

- Cool completely to make it easier to remove from the pan. Alternatively, you can line the loaf pan with parchment paper.

Recipe Notes

- If you would like to make a glaze for your lemon poppy seed loaf simply mix together a powdered sweetener with lemon juice.

Nutrition Info

- Calories 176 Calories from Fat 117
- Total Fat 13g 20%
- Saturated Fat 4g 20%
- Cholesterol 66mg 22%
- Sodium 108mg 5%
- Potassium 130mg 4%
- Total Carbohydrates 7g 2%
- Dietary Fiber 3g 12%
- Sugars 1g
- Protein 7g 14%

93. Broccoli & Cheddar Keto Bread Recipe

This Broccoli & Cheddar Keto Bread Recipe is a great breakfast, lunch, side dish, or snack. It mixes up in 5 minutes and has only 5 ingredients plus salt. It is nut free, grain-free, gluten-free, and a THM S. It also reheats well on busy mornings.

Prep Time 5 mins
Cook Time 30 mins
Total Time 35 mins
Servings: 10 slices

Ingredients

- 5 eggs beaten
- 1 cup shredded cheddar cheese
- 3/4 cup fresh raw broccoli florets chopped
- 3 1/2 tbsp coconut flour
- 2 tsp baking powder
- 1 tsp salt

Instructions

- Preheat oven to 350. Spray a loaf pan with cooking spray.
- Mix all the ingredients in a medium bowl. Pour into the loaf pan.
- Bake for 30-35 minutes or until puffed and golden. Slice and serve.
- To Reheat: Microwave or heat in a greased frying pan.

Nutrition Info

- Calories 90 Calories from Fat 54
- Total Fat 6g 9%
- Saturated Fat 3g 15%
- Cholesterol 93mg 31%
- Sodium 342mg 14%
- Potassium 164mg 5%
- Total Carbohydrates 2g 1%
- Dietary Fiber 1g 4%
- Protein 6g 12%

94. Turmeric Cauliflower Buns

These 4-Ingredient Turmeric Cauliflower Buns are an easy grain-free, low-carb, and super healthy side dish.

Prep Time: 30 mins
Cook Time: 30 mins
Serving: 6 1

Ingredients

- 1 medium head of cauliflower or about 2 cups of firmly packed cauliflower rice (see directions for making the cauliflower rice)
- 2 eggs
- 2 tablespoons coconut flour
- ¼ teaspoon ground turmeric
- pinch each of salt and pepper

Instructions
- Preheat oven to 400°F.
- Line a baking sheet with parchment paper and set aside.
- Take your cauliflower and use a sharp knife to cut off the base. Pull off any green parts and use your hands to break the cauliflower into florets. Give the florets a quick rinse and pat dry.
- Next, make cauliflower rice by placing the florets into the bowl of a food processor with the "S" blade. Pulse for about 30 seconds until the cauliflower is about the size of rice. You should have about two cups of firmly packed cauliflower rice.

- Place the cauliflower rice into a microwavable-safe bowl with about a teaspoon of water. Cover with plastic wrap and poke a few holes to let the steam escape. Microwave the cauliflower rice for about 3 minutes. Alternatively, you can steam the cauliflower rice on the stovetop in a steamer basket.
- Uncover the bowl and let the cauliflower rice cool for about 5 minutes. Then, use a large spoon to put the cauliflower rice into a nut milk bag or a clean dish towel. Squeeze the excess moisture out, being careful not to burn your hands.
- Pour the cauliflower rice into a medium mixing bowl and stir in the eggs, turmeric, and a pinch of salt and black pepper.
- Use your hands to form the mixture into 6 buns, placing them on the baking sheet.
- Bake for 25-30 minutes or until the top becomes slightly browned.
- The cauliflower buns are best served hot right out of the oven. They do not refrigerate or re-heat well (they will get mushy), but they are so delicious that you'll no doubt eat them right away!

Nutrition info

- Calories Per Serving: 59
- % Daily Value
- 3% Total Fat 2.1g
- 21% Cholesterol 62mg
- 6% Sodium 151.7mg
- 2% Total Carbohydrate 6.6g

95. Low Carb Keto Banana Walnut Bread

This recipe for low carb keto banana walnut bread uses a mixture of yellow squash and banana extract to mimic the taste of bananas.

Prep Time: 20
Cook Time: 1:00
Total Time: 1 hour 20 minutes
Serving: 12 slices

Ingredients

- cooking spray
- 1 cup super fine almond flour
- 1 cup flaxseed meal
- 3/4 cup Swerve or equivalent granulated sweetener
- 1/4 cup Isopure Whey Protein Powder or equivalent zero carb protein powder
- 1/4 cup oat fiber
- 1 tablespoon baking powder
- 1 teaspoon ground cinnamon
- 1/4 teaspoon salt
- 3 oz yellow squash (1/2 a squash), grated
- 5 large eggs
- 1 cup whole milk ricotta cheese
- 2 teaspoons vanilla extract
- 4 teaspoons banana extract
- 1/4 cup walnuts, chopped

Instructions

- Preheat oven to 350 degrees F. Cut a piece of parchment paper to fit in and over the side of a loaf pan. You'll use it to remove the bread to cool. Spray with non-stick cooking spray.

- In medium sized mixing bowl, add almond flour, flaxseed meal, sweetener, whey protein, oat fiber, baking powder, cinnamon and salt. Whisk together.

- Grate the yellow squash and blot the liquid from it with paper towels. Add to a large bowl along with eggs, ricotta cheese, vanilla and banana extract. Mix well to combine.

- Add the dry ingredients to the wet ingredients and mix well.

- Add batter to prepared loaf pan and use a spatula to smooth the top. Sprinkle walnuts over the top of the batter.

- Bake for 55-65 minutes until browned on top and a toothpick in the middle comes out clean. Check in at minute 40 and place a sheet of aluminum foil over the top to prevent further browning.

- Cool for 10 minutes in the pan. Cut around the edges of the pan and remove the loaf using the sides of parchment paper. Place loaf on cooling rack and cool for at least 10 more minutes before cutting.

Nutrition Info

- Calories: 193
- Fat: 14
- Carbohydrates: 9
- Fiber: 5
- Protein: 10

96. 3-Ingredient Grain-Free Bagels

Prep/Cook Time: 30 mins

Ingredients

- 3 eggs (organic and fresh!)
- 1/4 c. yogurt or sour cream (use dairy-free yogurt, if necessary)
- 1 1/2 c. almond flour

Instructions

- Preheat oven to 350 and grease 5 wells in a donut pan. (I use this donut pan.)

- Using a hand mixer, beat the eggs until they're light and creamy. Stir in the yogurt or sour cream until smooth.

- Slowly fold in the almond flour, 1/2 cup at a time.

- Spoon batter evenly into prepared donut molds and bake for 20 minutes.

- Slice, toast, and serve with butter, more sour cream, crème fraîche, coconut butter, whatever floats your boat!

97. Nearly No Carb Keto Bread

A zero carb bread is almost impossible to make. But, this low carb pork rind bread comes pretty close to being zero carb.

Prep Time 10 minutes
Cook Time 21 minutes
Total Time 31 minutes
Servings 12 people

Ingredients

- 8 ounces cream cheese
- 2 cups mozzarella cheese grated (about 210 grams)
- 3 large eggs
- 1/4 cup parmesan cheese grated (about 27 grams)
- 1 cup crushed pork rinds about 46 grams
- 1 tablespoon baking powder

Optional:

- herbs and spices to taste

Instructions

- Preheat oven to 375°F. Line baking sheet (I used a 12 x 17 jelly roll pan) with parchment paper.
- Place cream cheese and mozzarella cheese in large microwaveable bowl.
- Microwave cheese on high power for one minute, stir, then microwave for another minute and stir again. The cheese should be fully melted.
- Add egg, parmesan, pork rinds, and baking powder. Stir until all ingredients have been incorporated.
- Spread mixture onto parchment paper lined pan. Bake at 375°F for 15-20 or until lightly brown on top.
- Allow pan to cool on rack for 15 minutes, then remove bread from pan and cool directly on rack.
- Slice into 12 equal sized pieces. Can be eaten plain or used to make sandwiches.

Nutrition Info

- Calories 166 Calories from Fat 117
- Total Fat 13g 20%
- Saturated Fat 7g 35%
- Cholesterol 86mg 29%
- Sodium 294mg 12%
- Potassium 158mg 5%
- Total Carbohydrates 1g 0%
- Dietary Fiber 0g 0%
- Sugars 0g
- Protein 9g 18%

98. Keto Walnut Bread

Prep Time: 10 minutes
Cook Time: 40 minutes
Total Time: 50 minutes
Servings: 10 Slices

Ingredients

- 1/2 cup coconut flour
- 1 tablespoon baking powder
- 2 tablespoons psyllium husk powder
- 1/2 teaspoon salt
- 4 eggs
- 4 tablespoons olive oil or coconut oil
- 2 tablespoons apple cider vinegar
- 1 cup walnuts chopped
- 1/2 cup boiling water

Instructions

- Preheat the oven to 180C/350F degrees
- Place the coconut flour, baking powder, psyllium husk powder and salt in a bowl and mix thoroughly.
- Add the oil and eggs and blend well until the mixture looks like breadcrumbs.
- Add the apple cider vinegar and mix well.
- Add the chopped walnuts to the bread and mix.
- Gently add the water, a bit at time and stir into the mixture (you may not need it all).

- Line a baking tray with parchment paper.
- Using your hands, make a large ball of the dough (I find keeping my hands wet helps with the sticky dough).
- Place the dough on the parchment paper lined baking tray.
- Score the top to make a pattern (optional but looks more rustic)
- Bake for 35 -40 minutes until golden and firm.
- Slice, eat and enjoy!

Nutrition Info
- Calories: 188kcal
- Carbohydrates: 7.3g
- Protein: 5g
- Fat: 16g
- Fiber: 4.3g

99. Gluten Free, Paleo & Keto Drop Biscuits

Ultra tasty, easy, tender and moist. These gluten free, paleo and keto drop biscuits check all the right boxes! Whip them up in 30, for an awesome low carb bread that goes great with sweet and savory alike.

Prep Time: 10 minutes
Cook Time: 20 minutes
Total Time: 30 minutes
Servings: biscuits

Ingredients

- 1 egg
- 77 g sour cream or coconut cream + 2 tsp. apple cider vinegar, at room temp
- 2 tablespoons water
- 1 tablespoon apple cider vinegar
- 96 g almond flour
- 63 g golden flaxseed meal or psyllium husk, finely ground
- 21 g coconut flour
- 20 g whey protein isolate or more almond flour
- 3 1/2 teaspoons baking powder
- 1 teaspoon xanthan gum or 1 TBS. flaxseed meal
- 1/2 teaspoon kosher salt
- 112 g organic grass-fed butter or 7 TBS. ghee/coconut oil

Instructions

- Preheat oven to 450°F/230°C. Line a baking tray with parchment paper or a baking mat.

- Add eggs, sour (or coconut) cream, water and apple cider vinegar to a medium bowl and whisk for a minute or two until fully mixed. Set aside.

- Add almond flour, flaxseed meal, coconut flour, whey protein, baking powder, xanthan gum (or more flax) and kosher salt to a food processor and pulse until very thoroughly combined.

- Add in the butter and pulse a few times until pea-sized. Pour in the egg and cream mixture, pulsing until combined. The dough will be very shaggy.

- Drop 6 rounds of dough onto the prepared baking tray. Brush with melted butter and bake for 15-20 minutes until deep golden. Allow to cool for 10 minutes before serving. These guys keep well, stored in an airtight container at room temperature, for 3-4 days.

- You can freeze the shaped biscuit dough for 1-2 months, and bake straight from the freezer as needed.

Nutrition Info
- Calories 290 Calories from Fat 270
- Total Fat 30g 46%
- Saturated Fat 11g 55%
- Cholesterol 74mg 25%
- Sodium 455mg 19%
- Potassium 113mg 3%
- Total Carbohydrates 8g 3%
- Dietary Fiber 5g 20%
- Sugars 1g
- Protein 7g 14%

100. Turmeric Cauliflower Buns

These 4-Ingredient Turmeric Cauliflower Buns are an easy grain-free, low-carb, and super healthy side dish.

Prep Time: 30 mins
Cook Time: 30 mins
Serving: 6

Ingredients

- 1 medium head of cauliflower or about 2 cups of firmly packed cauliflower rice (see directions for making the cauliflower rice)
- 2 eggs
- 2 tablespoons coconut flour
- ¼ teaspoon ground turmeric
- pinch each of salt and pepper

Instructions

- Preheat oven to 400°F.
- Line a baking sheet with parchment paper and set aside.
- Take your cauliflower and use a sharp knife to cut off the base. Pull off any green parts and use your hands to break the cauliflower into florets. Give the florets a quick rinse and pat dry.
- Next, make cauliflower rice by placing the florets into the bowl of a food processor with the "S" blade. Pulse for about 30 seconds until the cauliflower is about the size of rice. You should have about two cups of firmly packed cauliflower rice.

- Place the cauliflower rice into a microwavable-safe bowl with about a teaspoon of water. Cover with plastic wrap and poke a few holes to let the steam escape. Microwave the cauliflower rice for about 3 minutes. Alternatively, you can steam the cauliflower rice on the stovetop in a steamer basket.
- Uncover the bowl and let the cauliflower rice cool for about 5 minutes. Then, use a large spoon to put the cauliflower rice into a nut milk bag or a clean dish towel. Squeeze the excess moisture out, being careful not to burn your hands.
- Pour the cauliflower rice into a medium mixing bowl and stir in the eggs, turmeric, and a pinch of salt and black pepper.
- Use your hands to form the mixture into 6 buns, placing them on the baking sheet.
- Bake for 25-30 minutes or until the top becomes slightly browned.
- The cauliflower buns are best served hot right out of the oven. They do not refrigerate or re-heat well (they will get mushy), but they are so delicious that you'll no doubt eat them right away!

Nutrition Info

- Calories Per Serving: 59
- % Daily Value
- 3% Total Fat 2.1g
- 21% Cholesterol 62mg
- 6% Sodium 151.7mg
- 2% Total Carbohydrate 6.6g

CONCLUSION

Ketogenic diets offer a host of unique benefits that cannot be ignored if you are chasing the ultimate, low bodyfat figure or physique. However, they are not the most user friendly of diets and any 'middle ground' compromise you might prefer will be just the worst of all worlds. Your choice is to do them right or not at all.

Manufactured by Amazon.ca
Bolton, ON